A ... n
OF
Jewish Parents

Also by Anna Sequoia

The Official J.A.P. Handbook

The Official J.A.P. Paper Doll Book (with Patty Brown)

67 Ways to Save the Animals

No Bad Men (with Sarah Gallick)

Chunks (with Patty Brown)

The Complete Catalog of Mail Order Kits

Backpacking on a Budget (with Steven Schneider)

The Climbers Sourcebook (with Steven Schneider)

Adult Children

OF

Jewish Parents

The _Last_ Recovery Program You'll Ever Need

Anna Sequoia

(née Schneider)

Crown Trade Paperbacks
New York

Copyright © 1993 by Anna Sequoia

Published by Crown Publishers, Inc., 201 East 50th Street, New York,
New York 10022. Member of the Crown Publishing Group.

Random House, Inc. New York, Toronto, London, Sydney, Auckland

Crown Trade Paperbacks and colophon are trademarks of Crown
Publishers, Inc.

Manufactured in the United States of America

Library of Congress Cataloging-in-Publication Data
Sequoia, Anna.
Adult children of Jewish parents : the last recovery program
you'll ever need / by Anna Sequoia. —1st ed.
p.   cm.
1. Jews—United States—Humor.   I. Title.
PN6231.J5S39   1993
818'.5402—dc20   93-3966
CIP

ISBN 0-517-88116-0

10 9 8 7 6 5 4 3 2 1

First Edition

ACKNOWLEDGMENTS

For their enthusiasm and assistance, I would like to thank Sharon Beitz, Ward Calhoun, Molly Colliton, Neil Hart, Keith Moskowitz, Sharon O'Shea, Bushey Schneider, Judy Schneider, Peggy Schneider, and Larry Stein. Special thanks to John Boswell, Patty Brown, Patricia Conoway, and Erica Marcus.

THE ADULT CHILD OF JEWISH PARENTS CREDO

I am, therefore
I am entitled.

CONTENTS

INTRODUCTION

Carla Jung,
M.D., P.C., Ph.D.

As the 1980s were the decade of Wall Street and greed, the 1990s seem to be shaping up as the decade of recovery. Virtually everyone, it seems, is either championing his or her inner child, in the process of becoming co-dependent no more, or meditating so that she (or he) can stop doing too much.

Naturally, as one of the most media-savvy psychotherapists in America, through my many years of practice and appearances on Phil, Oprah, and Joan, I have personally seen many of these people . . . quite a few of whom happen to be Adult Children of Jewish Parents.

Yet the frustrating thing has always been that despite my expert therapeutic skills, combined with my patients' dedicated attendance at conventional 12 Step meetings, many of my clients seemed to be making little progress. In fact, some patients were quite clear about the fact that existing 12 Step programs didn't seem quite right for them—but they weren't exactly sure why.

And then I heard about the ingenious work of Dr. Sequoia. She had reached many of the same roadblocks with her patients. But unlike those of us in the therapeutic community who were still concentrating on dream symbolism, for example, or pining for the golden days of the great cult of neurosis, Dr. Sequoia was taking a more pragmatic approach. And achieving remarkable success.

Through her own recovery experience, as she has explained to me through our continuing conversations, many of which are available on videotape, she had been forced to come to the following conclusions:

• No matter how fashionable it may be to attend a conventional 12 Step program these days, meetings are held in rooms that are sorely in need of interior decoration. Jewish people—sensitive Jewish women in particular—simply do not recover from psychological problems in bare storefronts or the back rooms of churches. That's just a fact of life, as we know it.

• Meetings are nominally free, although generally participants stick a dollar bill into an ugly basket passed around the room. Yet it is a well-known fact that Jewish people do not recover from psychological problems unless they pay a therapist the equivalent of a down payment on a condo.

• AA, OA, and other recovery groups expect each person who attends to hold hands with strangers. Holding hands with strangers is simply not part of American Jewish culture (unless participants have attended ultra-Reform congregations in Maryland or Virginia that share facilities with Unitarians).

• There are extremely inadequate refreshments, if any.

• But most important, conventional 12 Step programs place a great deal of emphasis on a "Higher Power." Although there is a lot of shilly-shallying about the nature of this Higher Power, most successful 12 Step participants tend to see this Higher Power as a dominant male God-force. Naturally this is totally out of the question for Jewish people, where dominant males exist only among Hasidim.

It was commonsense observations like these that encouraged Dr. Sequoia to found the Institute for Adult Children of Jewish Parents nearly a decade ago.

Clearly there was a need: through the years, thousands of ACoJPs have passed through the institute's centers in New York, Atlanta, Santa Fe, Winnetka, Boulder, St. Bart's, and Los Angeles. And by next fall a new facility, the Ralph Lauren Adult Children of Jewish Parents Recovery and Ski Center, will be ready to open in Aspen.

And now, because of the importance of the work—and because not everyone has the time or resources to participate in the institute directly—here at last is the "Big Book" Adult Children of Jewish Parents have so long needed . . . and deserved. The book so many of us in the psychotherapeutic community have encouraged and (just a bit) dreaded:

ADULT CHILDREN OF JEWISH PARENTS:

The Last Recovery Program You'll Ever Need.

I

ARE YOU AN ADULT
CHILD OF
JEWISH PARENTS?
A Simple Diagnostic Exercise

1. I feel that the best way to deal with my parents is to
a. move between 50 and 100 miles away.

b. move between 500 and 1,000 miles away.

c. move to another coast.

d. move to another country.

2. A pint of Häagen-Dazs is
a. one of the greatest cultural developments of the twentieth century.

b. a single serving–size container.

c. a simple way to cure virtually any problem.

d. all of the above.

3. My brother (or sister) and I
a. are warm, close personal friends.

b. each have a key to our parents' safe-deposit box.

c. never compete with each other.

d. would never have chosen to have anything to do with each other, if we didn't happen to be related.

4. Whenever something bad happens I call my mother, because
a. she'll tell me how wonderful I am and what jerks the other people must be.

   b. she'll help me realize that whatever happened, it must be my fault.

   c. she'll tell me how much better everyone else's children are doing.

   d. I never learn.

5. One of my fondest fantasies is that I win
   a. the right to sue anyone I want, without charge.

   b. the Miss America contest, so I can be the second Jewish Miss America.

   c. a date with Sammy "the Bull" Gravano.

   d. the lottery.

6. If I were stranded on a desert island, I would most want to have
   a. a change of underwear.

   b. sun block, SPF 15 or higher.

   c. George Stephanopoulos.

   d. my mommy.

7. I am currently not speaking to
   a. at least one relative.

   b. two or more relatives.

   c. anyone on my father's (or mother's) side of the family.

   d. my cat.

8. The reason I stay in my current job, even though I hate it, is
   a. there could be another Depression.

   b. I can retire in another twenty-one years with a good pension.

   c. change gives me a stomachache.

   d. who else would hire me?

9. I really have to try to be nicer to my mother, because
   a. she's liable to die young, of a stroke, like her mother did.

   b. she sacrificed so to help me get where I am today.

   c. she stayed with my father all those years and gave me a stable home life—not like all these young women today.

   d. she told me to.

10. For my fortieth birthday, I would like
   a. a trip to the Golden Door spa.

   b. my thighs and/or eyes done.

   c. a richer, sexier husband.

   d. all of the above.

11. I'd say my mother most resembles
   a. Donna Reed on "The Donna Reed Show."

   b. Dottie in *This Is My Life.*

   c. Gertrude Berg in "The Molly Goldberg Show."

   d. Norma Desmond in *Sunset Boulevard.*

   e. Don't ask. . . .

How to Calculate Your Score

Award yourself 5 points for each correct answer, except where otherwise indicated:

1. b), c), or d) are correct; a)—as you will find out—is rarely far enough.

2. a), b), or c) are correct; d), however, is most correct and rates 25 points.

3. a) and b) are correct; d) rates 25 points. If you answered c), you are either in denial or not of the Jewish persuasion.

4. b), c), or d) are correct.

5. a), b), c), or d).

6. a), b), c), or d).

7. a) or b) are correct; c) rates 25 points.

8. a), b), c), or d).

9. a), b), c), or d).

10. a), b), or c); d) rates 25 points.

11. e) is correct.

What Your Score Means

125 Points or More—You need to read and study this recovery program *as soon as possible.*

25–125 Points—Recovery is just around the corner. So sit, get yourself a nice snack—and read this book.

Less than 25 Points—That's the best you could score? Your cousin Marlene, you know, got a *much* higher score. . . . You'd better turn to page 15—and start reading.

II

WHAT HAPPENED TO YOU AS A CHILD?

When is a child not a child? When that child lives with Jewish parents. But, more correctly, when is a child not childlike? You certainly looked like a child and dressed like a child (in fact, your mother dressed you extremely well as a child). Others may have seen you as a child, but that was because they missed the look of worry on your tiny face.

In fact, you were the pure, sweet child of fairy tales. Bright eyes. Shining hair that glinted red in the sun. Your mind and heart were open.

You were so receptive to education. Books were a mystery, a magical challenge you readily solved. They took you to the land of Pharoah. They transported you to ancient Rome.

Each day was an adventure, a time to laugh, to play with friends. As long as you were young and relatively quiet, you were loved. You were a prince. A princess.

And then it all gradually began. . . . Perhaps you were mocked for not learning to ride a bike easily. Or your first B + was cause for derision. Or you were dressed in orthopedic oxfords and made to wear them to school as well as to family parties.

ADULT CHILDREN OF JEWISH PARENTS

David (Son of Sam) Berkowitz

Sigmund Freud

Barbra Streisand

Bess Myerson

Sukhreet Gabel

Jesus of Nazareth

Harvey Fierstein

Woody Allen

Mayor Ed Koch

Howard Stern

Norman Mailer

Sandra Bernhard

Dr. Ruth

Richard Lewis

Philip Roth

David Lee Roth

Erica Jong

Julian Schnabel

Neil Simon

Ronald Lauder

Barry Manilow

Bob Dylan

Marcel Proust

Frances Lear

Senator Arlen Specter

Fran Lebowitz

Michael Douglas

Roseanne Arnold

Joan Rivers

Melissa Rivers

Jeffrey Katzenberg

Elayne Boosler

David Liederman

Kevin Maxwell

"Crazy" Eddie Antar

Cindy Adams

Calvin Klein

Adrien Arpel

HONORARY ADULT CHILDREN
OF JEWISH PARENTS

Paul Prudhomme   *Roger Clinton*

Dom DeLuise   *Connie Chung*

Luciano Pavarotti

A little brother or sister was born—and no one any longer seemed to want to see you dance or sing your songs. In gym you may have been one of the last picked to be on a team. In camp, when boys and girls began to pair off together, you were left with the quiet, nail-biting kids, the kids with braces on their teeth and eyeglasses. The children who looked as if they were going to grow up to look like Woody Allen—or Bette Midler.

That's how you were treated if, like little Sheila Gold, you were considered the perfect child, the star of the family—the "genius."* Imagine if you'd been anything less. . . .

To an outsider looking in, you were simply a smart, cute child with a hefty layer of baby fat. And, of course, that *was* the case. They just didn't see the whole picture. . . . But, then, perhaps you had another role in the family. Perhaps you were the "dummy"*—the one with learning disabilities. People would say, "Look at Eric, it's such a shame. Mrs. Gold's brother, Solly, was like that. He wound up at Daitch-Shopwell, slicing lox. Eric must have gotten it from him. What a pity."

If you were Eric, what did you feel? Perhaps you didn't allow yourself to feel. Or perhaps you escaped into elaborate fantasies, in which you stood on the roof of your apartment building or, if you grew up in suburbia, a nearby mall. In your hands would be a very big, very powerful rifle, and in that fantasy

*For an examination of the role you—or someone you know—may have played in *your* (or his or her) family, please see the genogram on page 36: "Sheila Gold's Dysfunctional Jewish Family."

you would shoot at anyone you felt like getting even with, especially your mother or Aunt Helen.

But that was perfectly normal. . . . You were simply a misunderstood little boy, just beginning a lifetime of *tsouris*—and therapy. A lifetime as an Adult Child of Jewish Parents.

Or perhaps you were more like Lawrence Gold, the "straight arrow"*—whose every action, every thought, was a compromise. You got straight A's in school. But everyone suggested that that was because you were so diligent and studied so hard. Unlike Sheila, you could *not* have been a "genius"—or even particularly gifted or smart; that wasn't your role.

Yet you were such a good boy. You dressed neatly and conservatively, even in junior high school. Outwardly you concerned yourself with the acquisition of things: getting the best sound system available or the best camera and lenses. There was never any doubt that you'd be admitted to medical school. The question was simply where, which one.

But inside, how did you feel? Did you believe that everyone else was growing up with the same kind of nervous stomach? Did you think that every other little boy carried a Ventolin inhaler and every day took Theo-Dur? Did you believe it was normal to suppress all your emotions?

And then there's Leah . . . or is it Staci Anne Gold? You know who you are—the awkward but rather pretty little child drawing quietly in her room or watching TV silently. Everyone else in the family is so brilliant—or so much trouble. It seems like there's never much of anything left for you. That's why you always see yourself as—and really are—the "orphan" child, hoping for some attention but always in the shadow.

Let's face it. Life at home in your American Jewish household was not always a bowl of latkes. . . .

TOXIC JEWISH MOTHERS

Hollywood Division

Jolie Gabor

Shelley Winters

Totie Fields

Milton Berle

Larger Than Life

Leona Helmsley

Helena Rubinstein

Lillian Vernon

Roseanne Arnold

Literary Division

Sophie Portnoy

Isadora Wing

Special Cases

Hedda Nussbaum

Judge Hortense Gabel

Historical Division

Rebecca   Mary   Golda Meir

TOXIC JEWISH FATHERS

Meyer Lansky

David Levine

God, the Father

Job

John Gutfreund

Rupert Murdoch

HOME LIFE

Adult Children of Jewish Parents all grew up in similar environments. It doesn't matter if you grew up on West End Avenue or Myrtle Avenue, in Cleveland, Connecticut, Cedarhurst, or Los Angeles; what happened to you there was in many ways the same.

Remember what it was like at home? Close your eyes for a moment. Think of what it looked like. Now, in your mind, enter the foyer or vestibule. That's it. Don't be afraid; your mother's in the kitchen and won't know you're in the house.

Walk into the living room. Have you taken off your shoes so that you don't get schmutz on the carpeting? That's good. Now, go over to the couch and sit down. Rest for a few moments. Are you sticking to the plastic cover yet? Or is yours the type of home in which the couch is covered in an attractive, chic floral print?

Just relax. And try to remember. What do you hear? Is the TV on? Is the radio in the kitchen tuned to an all-news station? Can you hear your mother washing dishes in the sink while she talks on the phone to Aunt Adele? And what is she saying? Is it something nice about someone you know?

Of course it isn't. . . . But stay in the moment. The important thing is, what do you feel? How does it feel to be sitting in the living room where you grew up? Do you feel all warm and cozy and safe? Is it the kind of place you think about when you think about planning a vacation? Or are you perhaps getting a slight headache? Are you suddenly extremely, ravenously hungry? Do you feel as though you might jump out of your skin if you don't eat something with a good deal of sugar in it right away?

Just don't worry yourself. . . . Relax.

Here comes your mother, carrying a nice snack for you. . . . Perfect: cake.

Are you a bit confused?

Did you think you could actually sit alone in the living room of the house or apartment where you grew up and have any privacy, even reading, as an adult, about a recovery program you so badly need? Did you actually harbor the notion, even for a single moment, that your mother wouldn't know *exactly* what you were thinking—that in your mind, at least, you were finally home for a visit?

Do you think you can ever effectively escape from your mother? What are you, meshuga?

FAMOUS JEWISH CO-DEPENDENTS

Elizabeth Taylor	*Nicky Hilton*
	Mike Todd
	Richard Burton
	John Warner
Eddie Fisher	*Elizabeth Taylor*
Debbie Reynolds	*Eddie Fisher*
Carrie Fisher	*Paul Simon*
Henry Kissinger	*Richard Nixon*
Gertrude Stein	*Alice B. Toklas*
Sammy Davis, Jr.	*Peter Lawford*
	Frank Sinatra
	Dean Martin
Jerry Lewis	*Dean Martin*
Virginia Woolf	*Leonard Woolf*
Martha Gelhorn	*Ernest Hemingway*
Arthur Miller	*Marilyn Monroe*
Carl Bernstein	*Nora Ephron*

Now, Adult Children of Jewish Parents will sometimes go to great lengths to try to escape the trauma of their past. They will move to another state. They will change their names. They will date and marry into another religion and/or culture, in the hope that they can make a new beginning.

As one client at the Institute for Adult Children of Jewish Parents, Sue R., put it recently:

I met Leon, who's half French, half Cherokee, at a gallery opening in SoHo. I guess I was drawn to him because of his exotic look and long hair. I always have favored a man with hair down past his shoulders. My dad, Lou, just has a fringe of hair above his ears and in a kind of horseshoe around his head, so I find a guy with hair attractive.

So Leon and I start to go out, and before long I discover that Leon has the largest male organ I have ever in my life encountered. I guess he or it was some kind of anomaly.

Anyway, we were spending a lot of time together, though the fact that he was making his living as a carpenter did kind of bother me; when we met, he had told me that he was an artist. But I guess not every artist can be as successful as Julian Schnabel. But I was trying to be supportive about it. He built some shelves for me in my apartment, which was pretty nice of him, and he also installed a new custom clothes rack system for me. I guess we found enough to talk about. That is, until I had that dream:

"I was at a hotel in the desert, maybe in Santa Fe. I was sitting in the hotel lounge, with friends of mine from college. And we were having a great time, laughing, drinking frozen margaritas without salt. There were holiday decorations all over the place, bunches of red glass chili peppers, and those lights, those little votive candles inside brown paper bags all along the tops of counters and shelves, and in some of the nichos.

And I'm feeling great, and suddenly Leon walks in, wearing payess and one of those long black wool coats and a hat like the Hasidim wear, and he's carrying a box of tools. He's come to fix the plumbing. And then he takes off the hat, and above the payess, all he has is this thin fringe of hair just

above his ears. And I realize, Hey, this isn't Leon anymore;
it's Lou. I swear: his face turned right into my father's face.
I woke screaming. It was one of the worst nightmares I'd
had in years. Naturally, I couldn't have anything to do with
Leon after that.

Sue R. was trying to escape. But the shadows of her early life
were coming back to haunt her. Yet once she began whole-
heartedly to dedicate herself to the 12 Step recovery program
developed at the Institute for Adult Children of Jewish Parents—developed specifically for people like *us*—her life has
become measurably, fulfillingly better.

SCHOOL

Your home life was bound to affect your performance at school.
How did you do in school? Do you look back at junior high
school as a high point of your adolescence? Will you always
think of high school as one of the best times of your life?

If you were like Lawrence, you probably did very well indeed. You studied hard. You made straight A's. You sprayed
that Ventolin inhaler. And you got into a good college.

But what if you were Eric, the "dummy"? Were you forced
to take an academic course anyway, so that your parents could
find a college—virtually any college—for you where you could
dictate your term papers into a tape recorder? Or were you
guided into a "trade" school, so that with your IQ of 154, you
could spend your young manhood installing linoleum or wall-
to-wall carpeting? And how did that feel?

Or perhaps you were more like Sheila, the "genius." Being a
genius, you would inevitably discover that because you *left* for
school didn't mean that you had to *go* to school. And it certainly didn't mean that after checking into homeroom, you had
to *stay* in school. Not when there were libraries and museums
that were that much more interesting. . . . Or simply friends to
see and cigarettes to smoke.

But then, brilliant and talented though you may have been,

your grade-point average began to slide. Vassar, unless you were a boy "genius," no longer was a possibility. You were guided toward "progressive" colleges—where young Adult Children of Jewish Parents didn't necessarily need a decent grade-point average to get in. And then you were schlepped to your first psychotherapist—who probably had no particular insight into your real problems, as he or she was undoubtedly also an unrecovered Adult Child of Jewish Parents.

And how did that feel? How did it feel to be such a disappointment?

Or perhaps you were more like little "orphan" Staci Anne . . . the child with just average grades and even less than average SATs. The child who, on her own, suddenly begins to blossom, insists upon going to the University of Wisconsin, or Alfred— and faster than anyone can blink an eye, winds up editing Martin Scorsese's films, or sells a series of photographs to the Museum of Modern Art.

"Gee, I never thought she was so talented," your mother will say in a daze. "Did you ever notice that she was so visual?" your bewildered mother will ask your cousin.

And how does *that* feel?

THE INSTITUTE FOR ADULT CHILDREN OF JEWISH PARENTS

Guide to Commonly Used Recovery Terms—and What They Mean for US

Easy Does It. An Adult Child of Jewish Parents can never take things too easy. Therefore, at the Institute for Adult Children of Jewish Parents, we heartily recommend naps. We also recommend several one-week vacations per year, one or more of which might well be at the institute's own recovery spa and hacienda in Santa Fe, New Mexico; our recovery and shiatsu massage center on the island of St. Bart's; or the Institute for Adult Children of Jewish Parents Yacht Club and Recovery Center, in Montauk, Long Island.

First Things First. An Adult Child of Jewish Parents can never be too careful about his or her personal hygiene. Thus, for purely therapeutic reasons, we highly recommend the purchase and use of a bidet.

Keep It Simple. Recovering ACoJPs have a certain resistance to removing the unwarranted jewel or home accessory. This is perfectly understandable, as the large majority have been raised with the philosophical premise that "more is more." Yet restraint is often the sad secret of elegance.

One Step at a Time. What you might be doing in a building without an elevator or an escalator is a bit of a mystery to us. But if circumstances are such that you must walk up steps, walk slowly, don't run, hold on to the railing, and be sure to rest every few steps.

Working the Steps. A linguistic and conceptual aberration that refers to the use of the StairMaster system of thigh and buttock control. ACoJPs would do well to avoid steps that lead nowhere.

Keep on Trying. One may not necessarily marry the first person with whom one lives. In fact, one may not even continue to live with the first person one marries. Therefore, an ACoJP would do well to invest her or his settlement wisely (keeping out enough, of course, for a nice extended bout of therapy)—and move on to the next mate.

No Pain, No Gain. This refers to the Jane Fonda exercise tapes. You may discard these. That's why God invented plastic surgery.

Some Are Sicker Than Others. Your sister-in-law, for example, or certain cousins.

In the Rooms. This of course refers to attending meetings. The rooms at each location of the Institute for Adult Children of Jewish Parents have been professionally decorated for your aesthetic and physical comfort by Mario Buatta and/or David Hundley or Judith Schneider.

Hide in the Rooms. In order to be sensitive to the needs of our vegetarian and animal rights activist clients, no fur or leather has been employed in the decoration of any rooms at any institute location.

Stay in Today. An excellent suggestion for those gray, chill winter days. There's no reason to go outside when it would really be so much pleasanter to curl up under the comforter with a good book, a nice cup of hot cocoa, and be cozy.

FRIENDS

What about friends? Did you have many?

Of course you didn't. You may have known quite a few children. After all, you went to school with them. You were in the same scout troop with them. You may all have taken tap or ballet lessons together. But even then you had essentially one or two "best" friends.

Usually your best friend was just like you. He or she lived in the same neighborhood, went to the same school, wore essentially the same clothing.

You played at each other's homes, although usually there was one home in which you felt just a little more comfortable, and you tried to go there. It was rarely *your* home. But even then you played quietly. If you lived in a house, you played downstairs, in the family room. And you were careful not to make too big a mess.

Of course, if your role in the family was the "dummy," like Eric, you probably *had* no friends. How could you? All day long in school you felt so different, so stupid. And after school you had to come right home so that your mother could sit you down in the kitchen with those delightful flash cards, so that she could finally shame you into learning to read.

But if you had a more normal role in the household, you gradually began to notice something remarkable: whenever you went over to your best friend's house, her mother always seemed to *like* you so much more than your own did. She always seemed so glad to see you. And she'd give you things: if you were a little hungry, a cupcake she made and decorated herself (and she didn't tell you you'd get fat if you ate it); if you were suddenly interested in geology, a sparkly piece of quartz she'd picked up during a vacation trip; if you especially liked pretty things, a handkerchief trimmed with tatted lace.

Sometimes, in fact, your friend said she thought her mother liked you more than she liked *her*.

Recently, when Hope B., a thirty-six-year-old recovering Adult Child of Jewish Parents, saw the mother of her best friend from the seventh grade in Loehmann's, in Havertown, Pennsylvania, it brought back a flood of memories. And she wrote this poem:

There you were at the sale rack outside the Back Room,
The diamonds and emerald of your engagement ring
Flashing like memory in the overhead fluorescent light.
You were always someone who could spot sterling
  mixed in a tray of silver plate.
It was you who first thought I was worth talking to.

I can't tell you now, looking back, how important it was
To be encouraged to sniff your bottle of Joy,
To try your Shalimar on my less than delicate wrists,
To be encouraged to put on those suede platform soles
  with ankle straps
And walk, as gracefully as possible, to the piano
Dressed in your best mink coat.

If today I am able to tell Meissen from Minton,
It is a tribute to you.
If today I am able to pull the one silk blouse from a
  rack full of polyester,
I owe it all to you.
If today I am able to remember my adolescence with
  any levity at all,
It is largely because of you.

Of course, like Hope B., you probably don't speak with your "best friend" from that age anymore. For that is the way it tends to be among unrecovered Adult Children of Jewish Parents: you have a best friend for a while, then move on. You argue with each other. Or you just seem to drift apart.

Unrecovered Adult Children of Jewish Parents have also been known to do this with wives or husbands.

III

ARE YOU AN ADULT CHILD OF JEWISH PARENTS?

Another Simple but Telling Diagnostic Exercise (for Women Only)

1. My sister-in-law thinks
   a. my brother was lucky to have grown up with a sister like me.
   b. I'm one of the finest human beings she's ever met.
   c. I am, basically, as bad as my mother.
   d. I *am* my mother.

2. Whenever I get sick, I think
   a. By tomorrow I'll feel a lot better.
   b. I'd better take a nice nap.
   c. Maybe I can get the Second Avenue Deli to send over some chicken soup (there's always Federal Express).
   d. It's fatal.

3. When it comes to investing, I
   a. make a concerted study of the market, then make my decision based upon what I think is right.
   b. depend quite a bit on the advice of my broker.
   c. keep my money in short-term CDs, so I can get my hands on it when I need it.
   d. would really prefer Daddy to do it.

4. If I could make myself sit through a movie based on my life, the title would be
   a. *Earth Girls Are Easy.*
   b. *Mildred Pierce.*

c. *Marjorie Morningstar.*

d. *Erotic in Nature.*

5. In my opinion, there's nothing like the clicking of
   a. castanets.

   b. call waiting.

   c. the shutter, as Annie Leibovitz photographs one for *Vanity Fair.*

   d. mah-Jongg tiles.

6. If I had to marry one of the following, in order to save my mother's life, my choice would be
   a. Jackie Mason.

   b. Albert Goldman.

   c. Charles Manson.

   d. Fran Lebowitz.

7. As a child, my mother's greatest fear was that I'd be
   a. fat.

   b. ugly.

   c. like my grandmother.

   d. unmarried.

8. The best thing about the neighborhood where I was raised was
   a. the proximity to fine appetizing stores.

   b. the informal, friendly people.

   c. sitting outside on the stoop in the summer.

   d. leaving it.

9. Liposuction is
   a. fine for some people, but not for me.

   b. the province of the insecure and the lumpy.

   c. quite a bargain, really, when you think about it.

   d. every American's birthright.

10. If I could say just one thing to my inner child, I would say, "Little _____ , you really have

    a. quite a pair of thighs on you."

    b. made a mess of things."

    c. come a long way, baby."

    d. turned out to be a magnificent—and exceptionally fabulous-looking—human being."

How to Score

Award yourself 5 points for every correct answer, except as indicated:

1. a) and b) rate 5 points each; c) deserves 10 points. If you checked d), you've reached the jackpot: 25 points.

2. a) and b) rate 5 points each. Again, c) deserves 10. And d): 25 points.

3. Same scoring as 1. and 2.

4. a), b), c), or d) = 25 points.

5. a), b), d) = 5 points; c) well deserves 25 points.

6. a) or b) = 5 points; d), a more sensible choice, rates 25 points.

7. a), b), or c) = 5 points; d), as you should have anticipated by now, rates 25.

8. b) or c) = 5 points. Either a) or d) = 25.

9. a) or c) = 5 points; d) = 25 points.

10. a) or b) or d) = 5 points.

How to Interpret Your Score

40 points or less—Obviously you are exhibiting resistance. Although this may be understandable, given your willful nature, you may want to take the test above one more time. . . .

50 to 70 points—Now we're talkin'! You are definitely an Adult Child of Jewish Parents. Nevertheless, provided you follow the program delineated in the pages that follow, your prognosis is excellent.

75 points to 125 points—Obviously you are an Adult Child of Jewish Parents *in extremis*. Your cure may cost a little more, you may need some time at our recovery center in St. Bart's, but if it's a cure you want, a cure you'll get. . . .

130 points or more—*Gottenyu!* You need some help as soon as possible. Perhaps you shouldn't wait to read the recovery program that follows. . . . You might be better off calling the Institute for Adult Children of Jewish Parents directly, for some *immediate* assistance. Our hot-line number, available twenty-four hours a day, is

1·800·TSOURIS

IV

THE DISEASE MODEL OF JEWISH PARENTING:

A Family Systems Approach, including How to Create a Genogram of Your Own Dysfunctional Jewish Family

Part of the job of any parent is to model behavior. It helps a child learn how to be a woman or how to be a man. It teaches us how to relate to each other: when to feel happy about another's success . . . when to use guilt or shame as methods of control . . . how to relate to storekeepers and the help . . . when, if ever, to give compliments.

From our primary caregivers (usually our parents, unless they have left us with a succession of Dominican or Peruvian baby-sitters and maids), we learn about the importance of milk and cookies as a way to cope with tension . . . the efficacy of taking to one's bed, alone, as a way of settling disputes . . . the fine art of withholding (affection, praise, cash) . . . and the importance of phoning home.

At the Institute for Adult Children of Jewish Parents, this last bit of behavior is a particular favorite of ours. We like to call it *enmeshment*. The way we see it, enmeshment does not refer to lycra—or lamé. Rather, as we define it, it refers to the little peculiarity in Jewish families of never truly letting their children go. Let's just call it

THE LAND OF EGYPT APPROACH TO CHILD REARING.

You may otherwise recognize this phenomenon as *taking an interest* or *being concerned*. Whatever one calls it, however, the bottom line is the same: no matter how far away you may move, no matter how you rebel or how traditional or untraditional your life-style may be, a Jewish parent *never willingly lets go.* But, then, neither did Pharoah. . . .

An important thing to remember is that for Adult Children of Jewish Parents, no matter what their age, and despite their own struggle to break free of their parents' control, patterns of dysfunction are *multigenerational.*

In chapter 2, as you may recall, we spoke briefly about the Golds, in particular about the structure of life within that family. You may recall little Sheila—the "genius"; Eric, the "dummy"; Lawrence, the "straight arrow," who went to medical school; and Staci Anne, the "orphan," who's now editing film for Martin Scorsese. All assigned roles.

Were Sheila, Eric, Lawrence, and Staci Anne the first people in their family to be assigned such roles? Of course not.

That's why, in our work at the institute, we find it extremely useful to create and study genograms of clients' families. Once you've studied the diagrams that follow, you may in fact want to replicate them, using material from your own family.

FIGURE 6.1 *Sheila Gold's Dysfunctional*

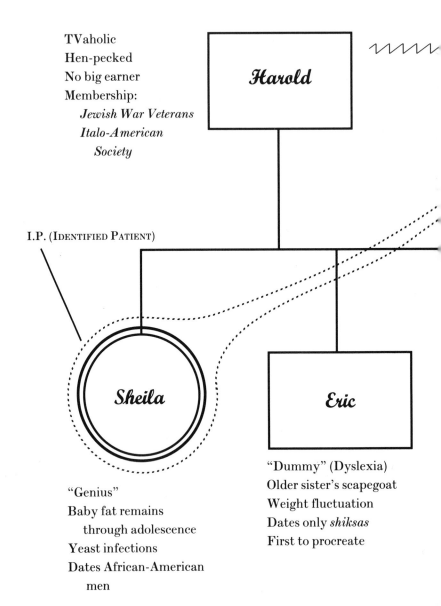

Jewish Family of Origin

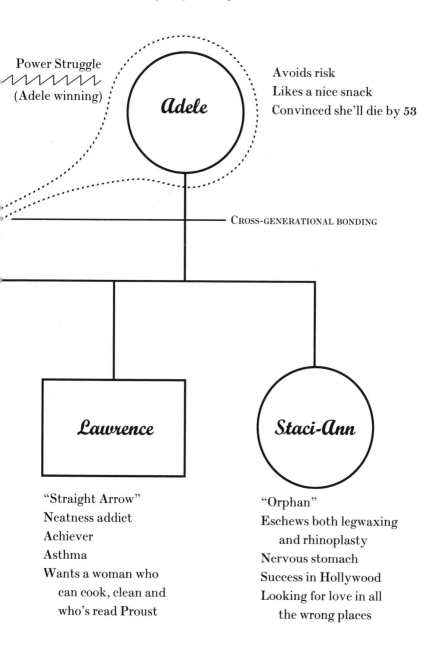

Power Struggle
(Adele winning)

Adele

Avoids risk
Likes a nice snack
Convinced she'll die by 53

CROSS-GENERATIONAL BONDING

Lawrence

"Straight Arrow"
Neatness addict
Achiever
Asthma
Wants a woman who
  can cook, clean and
  who's read Proust

Staci-Ann

"Orphan"
Eschews both legwaxing
  and rhinoplasty
Nervous stomach
Success in Hollywood
Looking for love in all
  the wrong places

FIGURE 6.2 *Sheila's Mother's*

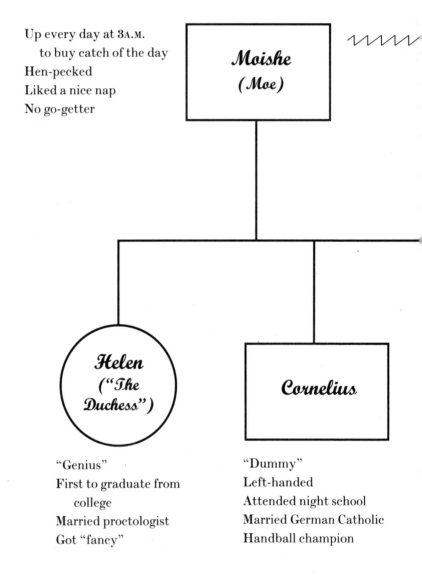

Up every day at 3A.M.
   to buy catch of the day
Hen-pecked
Liked a nice nap
No go-getter

Moishe (Moe)

Helen ("The Duchess")

"Genius"
First to graduate from
   college
Married proctologist
Got "fancy"

Cornelius

"Dummy"
Left-handed
Attended night school
Married German Catholic
Handball champion

(Adele's) Genogram

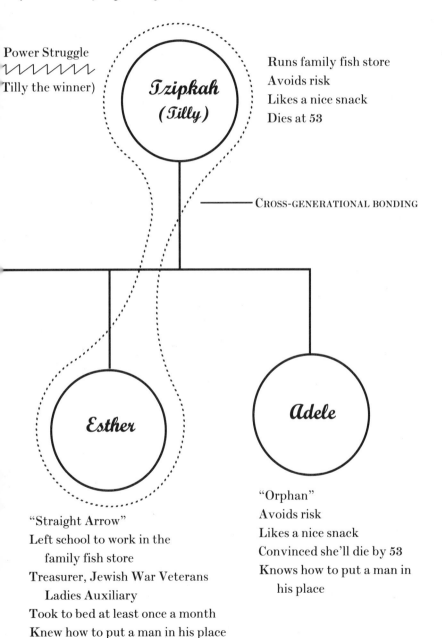

Power Struggle

Tilly the winner)

Tzipkah (Tilly)

Runs family fish store
Avoids risk
Likes a nice snack
Dies at 53

———— CROSS-GENERATIONAL BONDING

Esther

Adele

"Straight Arrow"
Left school to work in the
   family fish store
Treasurer, Jewish War Veterans
   Ladies Auxiliary
Took to bed at least once a month
Knew how to put a man in his place

"Orphan"
Avoids risk
Likes a nice snack
Convinced she'll die by 53
Knows how to put a man in
   his place

FIGURE 6.3 *Sheila's Father's*

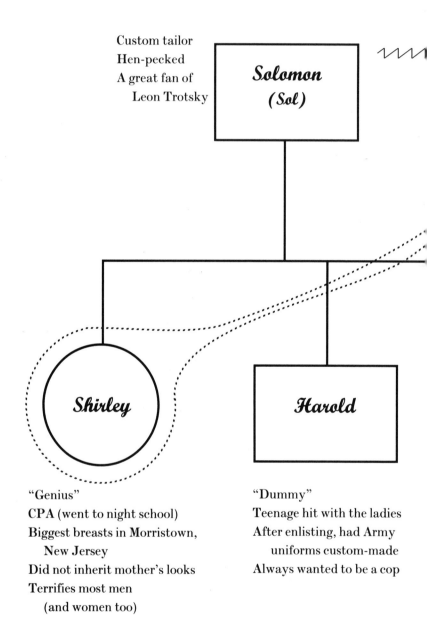

Custom tailor
Hen-pecked
A great fan of
Leon Trotsky

**Solomon
(Sol)**

Shirley

Harold

"Genius"
CPA (went to night school)
Biggest breasts in Morristown,
New Jersey
Did not inherit mother's looks
Terrifies most men
(and women too)

"Dummy"
Teenage hit with the ladies
After enlisting, had Army
uniforms custom-made
Always wanted to be a cop

(Harold's) Genogram

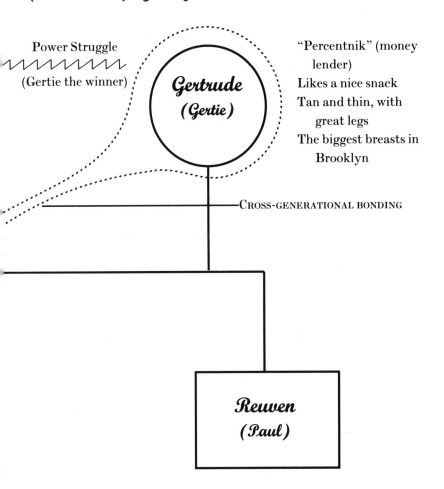

Power Struggle

(Gertie the winner)

Gertrude (Gertie)

"Percentnik" (money
    lender)
Likes a nice snack
Tan and thin, with
    great legs
The biggest breasts in
    Brooklyn

CROSS-GENERATIONAL BONDING

Reuven (Paul)

"Orphan"
Gave whole salary to his mom
    from ages 15–32
V.P., Accessories Division,
    Yves Saint Laurent
Tall and thin, with great legs
Lives with Ramon

V

WHAT IS HAPPENING TO YOU NOW?

There Is Healing in the Telling

The child of Jewish parents grows into an adult. But at what point? Is it the year you leave your parents' home to attend college? The year you take your first job? Your first apartment? Is it the day your first live-in lover leaves? The moment you acquire a pet?

For Adult Children of Jewish Parents, true adulthood begins at the precise moment your parents stop trying to run your life. Which, as we've seen in chapter 4, defines the problem: Jewish parents will never stop trying to run your life. They will never, as they say, stop "taking an interest" in you.

Adulthood, then, for Jewish people, is simply an arbitrary number assigned by statisticians.

Still, let us take a look at where you are today. . . .

1. ADULT CHILDREN OF JEWISH PARENTS ARE CAUTIOUS.

Here at the Institute for Adult Children of Jewish Parents,* we have developed many useful exercises for getting in touch with that wounded little person who still lives within you (your inner child). Please ask a friend to read these instructions to you while you do this exercise. Or, if you prefer, read these words into a tape recorder and play them back to yourself. . . .

*You can reach the Institute for Adult Children of Jewish Parents by dialing 1-800-TSOURIS.

*Close your eyes for a few moments. See yourself as a young
child. Try to remember a day when you were trying something
new for the first time: getting on roller skates, or diving into
a pool, or crossing a big street with two-way traffic. Remember
what kind of day it was. Was it sunny? . . . Good. How did
the sun feel on your arms, on your back, on your head? That's
right. . . . It feels warm and good. Now try to remember the
sounds. Breathe deeply and let your breathing help you feel
that child again. Concentrate on the sounds. What do you
hear? Is it a voice? Is it a frightened, shrill voice, saying,
"Careful!" "Don't!" "Watch it!" or "You'll get hurt"?*

*Is that what you hear? . . . That's okay. Relax. Feel the sun.
Now you can become your adult self again.*

As an Adult Child of Jewish Parents, you may have certain
cautionary messages that play when you deal with certain
types of risk-taking behavior.

As some clients at a recent sharing session of Adult Children
of Jewish Parents expressed it:

Judy: *"My boyfriend, Julio, says he's sick of fighting the
subway crowds in the morning and he wants to ride his
bicycle to work. I mean, I know that's a rational decision for
him to make, and ecologically responsible, but all I can see is
him crushed and dead under a truck. Every time he leaves the
house with the bike and the helmet, I'm convinced I'm going
to have to go down to the morgue to identify his body."*

Sharon: *"I didn't intend to spend the rest of my life eating
in the same three restaurants all the time, like my parents did,*

YOU'LL GET HURT!
(*Behavior Conscientious Jewish Mothers Would Have Forbidden*)

- Puberty

- Columbus's voyage into the unknown

- Charles Lindbergh's flight over water, especially at night

- Priscilla's moving in with Elvis at sixteen years old

- Sinéad O'Connor's shaving off all her hair

- Eddie Fisher's ever leaving Debbie

- Al Capone's neglect of his taxes

- E. L. Doctorow's decision to quit his job as an editor to write full-time

- Marie Curie working with radium

- Peter Arnett's remaining in Baghdad

- David Geffen's admission (to a New York paper, yet) that he dates men

---

but I like the Italian place, the bathrooms are clean, and the Indian restaurant is so inexpensive. It gives me a good choice of vegetarian dishes. And there's the take-out salad bar near work. . . . Okay, so that's really two restaurants. . . .*"

Dave: *"What I've always wanted to do is make it to the base camp of a climb up Mount Everest. I don't even think about going any farther than that, because I have asthma and I'm not a great climber anyway. But I'd just like to go, and see it all and be part of that atmosphere."*

Judy: *"It's like any time you love someone, you'll be punished by their being killed. . . ."*

Sharon: *"I don't even dwell on the possibilities—ptomaine, salmonella poisoning . . . I don't think that's the reason at all. I just feel so comfortable at my Italian restaurant. . . ."*

Dave: *"What I've done is make contributions toward the fund-raising efforts for climbs that interest me. . . ."*

Judy: *"When he leaves the apartment, I hear the sound of sirens."*

Sharon: *"I don't think there's any obligation to go beyond a certain distance away from home. Not unless you want to."*

Dave: *"At night, when I dream, I dream about mountains. . . . And it is not about my mother. I think about the Korakkoram the way some guys I know think about sex."*

Judy: *"All I can think about is the pain of the loss."*

Sharon: *"That was one of the reasons relocating was such a trauma. Eating out at new restaurants. Using new dry cleaners. Finding a new supermarket and new doctors. Change. Change is so unsettling. I gained thirty pounds when my company relocated me to Wilmington."*

Dave: *"I can't blame my parents for any of this, can I? It just seems like not realizing my dreams is part of my makeup."*

Judy: *"I make him call me when he gets to work."*

Sharon: *"I know it's a symptom, a symptom of other things. It's like part of the curse I carry from my mother's anxiety. Or is that overstating it? Am I being unfair?"*

Dave: *"Is this all there is?"*

Travel Tips for Reducing Anxiety
(*Mother's Nineteen Basic Rules*)

1. Be sure to pack extra underwear (including socks); there could be an emergency.

2. Take your hospitalization insurance card.

3. Make sure you have duplicates of all your prescriptions packed in separate bags.

4. If you are a parent, you and your spouse should never travel on the same plane.

5. Take a diarrhea medicine with you, just in case.

6. Avoid anything made with mayonnaise; you don't know how long it's been sitting without refrigeration.

7. Get to the airport at *least* two hours early.

8. Take some Ex-Lax with you, just in case.

9. Make sure you get a seat next to the emergency exit.

10. Don't drink any alcohol on the plane; you'll retain water.

11. A flashlight in your purse would be a very good idea. You'll need it, God forbid, in case of a crash.

12. Be sure to take your valuables with you when you go to the bathroom; thieves ride airplanes, too.

13. Wash your hands. Try not to touch anything in the bathroom when you're done. Opening the door with a paper towel is not a bad idea.

14. Be sure to take extra cash. But not too much cash.

15. Take traveler's checks. Leave the traveler's checks' numbers with Mother. Just in case.

16. Make sure each piece of luggage has a tag on it. Use your mother's phone number and *only* the city where you live.

17. Take credit cards. But not too many.

---

18. Call before you leave.

19. Call your mother as soon as you land. Then you can call your wife or husband.

---

2. ADULT CHILDREN OF JEWISH PARENTS ALWAYS LOOK ON THE BRIGHT SIDE.

Adult Children of Jewish Parents acknowledge that bad things can happen even to wonderful people. Especially if they are Jewish. So it is no wonder that Adult Children of Jewish Parents were not particularly surprised to learn, for example, that something as seemingly innocuous as taking a nice, relaxing sunbath, which makes you feel and look so good, can cause cancer. Or that a delicious potato kugel or a nice piece of corned beef can clog your arteries and make you drop dead right on the tennis court. What else is new?

That's why, as a diagnostic tool, the Institute for Adult Children of Jewish Parents uses the following simple, accurate test of just how bleak an ACoJP's worldview is (or is not). You will note that at the end of the test is a scoring guide, to help you determine both your diagnosis and your prognosis.

IT'S ALWAYS SOMETHING!
Yet Another Way of Diagnosing Yourself— And Saving a Few Dollars on Therapy
How to Determine Your Score

The checklist that follows will help determine just how bad off you might (or might not) be. Place a check in the box next to any problem or concern you had either today or within the past ten days. Then see the scoring guide that follows.

[ ] Woke with new wrinkle under right eye.

[ ] Pea under mattress kept me awake all night.

[ ] Boyfriend/girlfriend didn't call.

[ ] Son/daughter in college didn't call.

[ ] Mother didn't call.

[ ] Mother called.

[ ] Mother-in-law called.

[ ] If Andy and Fergie could break up, what's going to happen to us?

[ ] Now that beachfront property has gone down in price, I don't have the cash.

[ ] Must have been too much heat in the bedroom this morning; bedclothes kind of damp.

[ ] When you go to Venice on vacation and you order fish, does it come out of that polluted lagoon? What about when you go to France? Does the fish come out of the Mediterranean? Do you know what's *in* the Mediterranean?

[ ] If Marilyn Monroe were alive today, would she look like Shelley Winters?

[ ] What if it's not a recovery after all? What if it's another Depression?

[ ] If only my grandfather had founded Seagram's. . . .

[ ] It's about time I had a *big* diamond.

[ ] If I wear my fur coat, will those animal rights meshuggeners throw blood on me?

[ ] Who's to say Teflon doesn't cause those dark circles under the eyes?

[ ] What if my Joshua's school bus driver decides to hold the entire busload of kids for ransom? And then goes crazy from all the noise?

[ ] What if my husband insists I go to that convention in San Francisco with him—and that's when the Big One hits?

[ ] What if my therapist runs off with her psychic?

[ ] What if I can't get a cab, and the bus doesn't come, and I have to take a subway? Will I come down with a fatal case of drug-resistant TB?

[ ] What if William Kennedy Smith decides to specialize in OB/GYN?

[ ] What if I wind up as leathery and wrinkled as my paternal grandmother?

[ ] What if the plastic surgeon tells me he can't do anything for me? . . .

[ ] What if October 16 really *is* Armageddon?

How to Determine Your Score

Count the number of boxes in which you've placed checks; each check is worth 10 points.

10–30 points. You seem to have a certain amount of anxiety in your life. You could surely benefit from the appropriate 12 Step recovery program: this one.

40–60 points. Not only is your worldview a bit bleak, it's a wonder you're able to sleep at night. . . . In addition to participation in the appropriate 12 Step recovery program (this one), you may need some time at one of the inner child workshops offered at the Institute for Adult Children of Jewish Parents. For more information, please call 1-800-TSOURIS.

70 points or more. Oy, should you be worried. . . . You're a wreck. An extended journey aboard the Institute for Adult Children of Jewish Parents' upcoming luxury recovery cruise to Israel and the Greek islands is definitely in order. Please call immediately to register: 1-800-TSOURIS.

3. ADULT CHILDREN OF JEWISH PARENTS LIKE A NICE SNACK.

Food is, generally speaking, one of the greatest passions of the Adult Child of Jewish Parents. It is an interest that can, at times, supersede travel, friendship, romance, parenting, career, law and order, literature, world politics, shopping, and/or sex. As one client at the Institute for Adult Children of Jewish Parents phrased it succinctly in a revealing poem:

> *I think that there shall never be*
> *a kiss as sweet as Sara Lee,*
> *a hug as enticing*
> *as Häagen-Dazs ice cream,*
> *no love as stable*
> *as Nova, cream cheese, and a bagel.*
>   —ORIANA L.

Oriana, an attractive, slightly plump twenty-nine-year-old woman with a flourishing career in the travel industry, is an Adult Child of Jewish Parents whose family hails from Trieste, Italy, right near the border of the former Yugoslavia. Although both she and her family emigrated to this country during the late sixties, Oriana was lucky enough to have been exposed, at an impressionable early age, to the cuisines of three cultures. Recently, at a meeting of the Institute for Adult Children of Jewish Parents, she sat clutching her large, vintage Steiff teddy bear and shared her thoughts about some of the foods and food habits of her youth:

> *We always used to say to my mother that she could overfeed us in three languages. Sure, we made jokes about it, but neither my brother nor I ever missed a meal. The entertainment at my house was shopping for food, cooking the food, eating the food, reminiscing about that meal or other meals, and talking about ingredients we couldn't get here that we*

used to be able to get in Trieste. Like really ripe, sweet, succulent figs that burst open slightly when you touch them.

My mother made the best stews. My favorite is called *squazato*. She'd start off with a little fresh, unsalted butter and olive oil together, and add garlic, onion, and a little pork fat to it for flavor. (*Our family was never kosher*). Just as the onion would turn golden, everyone in the house would simultaneously begin salivating. Then she'd add the lamb, to brown it, seasoned with salt and pepper and a touch of cinnamon. Then some good, thick tomato paste, her homemade stock, and she'd cook it for hours.

We'd have that with polenta. Sometimes my mother would make her own bread, too, and that would drive me totally crazy. I'd dip the warm bread in the stew and feel like everything was right with the world, even though I guess it wasn't.

It wasn't until I moved into my own apartment, years later—against my parents' wishes, I might add—that I discovered I could get almost the same feeling of comfort and satisfaction from Chinese take-out, or Entenmann's crumb doughnuts—but only if I ate the whole box.

Food as comfort, food as love, seems a common, key experience among Adult Children of Jewish Parents. At a recent ACoJP workshop several ACoJPs discussed this very subject.

Mark: *"I really don't think I have any kind of a food problem. I'm just built big."*

Roberta: *"Well, I have a problem and I know it. I've been on every diet in America. I've gone on Optifast, Medifast, Slim-Fast, Weight Watchers, Diet Center, the Cathy Lee Crosby diet, and the one where they give you that dehydrated food. I even flew to Richmond to see someone at the Center for Holistic Healing. I've read Geneen Roth, and* Fat Is a

THE OFFICIAL ADULT CHILDREN OF JEWISH PARENTS GUIDE
to the Twenty-five Greatest Culinary Developments of the Twentieth Century

Decaf cappuccino

Home delivery of Chinese food

Microwave ovens

The Braun coffee bean grinder

Pepperidge Farm cookies

Heath toffee

Hellmann's mayonnaise

Entenmann's

Philadelphia light cream cheese

Focaccia

Equal

(The importation to this country of) De Cecco pasta

Ben & Jerry's Cherry Garcia

Julia Child

The New York Times Cookbook

Gael Greene

Next-day Air Express (now, even knishes can travel)

Snickers

Saga cheese

The Williams-Sonoma catalog

Optifast

Ex-Lax

Weight Watchers

Liposuction

THE OFFICIAL ADULT CHILDREN OF JEWISH PARENTS GUIDE TO
the Thirty-two Greatest (Nonculinary) Developments of the Twentieth Century

Frequent-flyer programs

Charge cards

Mail-order catalogs

VCRs

Four-wheel-drive automobiles

Nexxus Humectress shampoo

Telephone-answering machines

Call waiting

Beepers

Cellular telephones

Disposable diapers

Disposable contact lenses

CAT scans and MRIs

Shiatsu massage

Psychotherapy

Cetaphil lotion

Motrin

Underarm deodorant

The diaphragm

Loehmann's

Giorgio Armani

Donna Karan

Vogue and *HG*

Ever Clean cat litter

The Civil Rights movement

The Women's Movement

The Gay Rights Movement

The Rolodex

The early days of *New York* and *Vanity Fair*

Polio vaccine

Paperback books

Monistat cream

Health Insurance

Feminist Issue. *I went on that* fabulous *program where they tell you to get rid of your scale, go to the supermarket, and fill your cart with vast quantities of "forbidden" foods like Snickers, and Hershey's kisses, and Pepperidge Farm cookies. The idea is that you "decriminalize" those foods by always having them around. I gained fifteen pounds on that one. I* loved *that diet. . . ."*

Mark: *"My theory is there's no such thing as overeating; there's only underbuying. When I shop for food, anything that I can store or freeze I buy by the case."*

Melinda: *"I don't understand what the fuss is about. Anyone with a little self-discipline can be thin. Look at me, for example. I'm the thinnest person in this room. It's all a question of attitude. When I've eaten too much, I just throw up."*

Roberta: *"Uch!"*

Melinda: *"Or I use some of my frequent-flyer coupons and go down to Mexico for a couple of days. If you know where to go, you can get Desoxyn Gradumet and Preludin Endurets diet pills over the counter, without a prescription. . . . Can you imagine? I find that so civilized."*

Roberta: *"Right, and then you can get so wound up from them you wax the bathroom floor. . . ."*

Melinda: *"You're exaggerating. I haven't waxed the bathroom floor from taking diet pills in years. . . ."*

Mark: *"My mother always told me, 'Mark, it isn't worth having if it isn't worth having in multiples.' This way, if it's the middle of the night and I'm a little anxious, or in the mood for a snack, I have everything. I have pizza. I have bagels. I have chocolate-chip cookies. I have quarts of mayonnaise. I even have an emergency backup generator, in case there's a blackout; nothing in my house will ever spoil. . . ."*

Roberta: *"Right. You'd eat it all first. . . ."*

Melinda: *"Excuse me. Where's the bathroom?"*

Obviously this subject is fraught with emotional baggage (a forty-five-minute tape of this workshop is available, for $19.95 plus $3.50 postage and handling, from the Institute for Adult Children of Jewish Parents, 123 East 54 Street, Suite 8D, New York, NY 10022; please ask for Fat Workshop Tape #14).

The bottom line—and so often a wide one—is that Adult Children of Jewish Parents, given the right set of stressful circumstances, will for the rest of their lives periodically tend to dive into a vat of ice cream or a few tubs full of Chinese take-out. But recovery *is* possible, as you will see in chapter 8.

4. ADULT CHILDREN OF JEWISH PARENTS MAY EXPERIENCE AN OCCASIONAL HEADACHE

Adult Children of Jewish Parents have a great admiration for physicians. They like being them, they like marrying them, they like having them as fathers. They simply *kvell* at the thought of having one as a son or daughter, or son- or daughter-in-law. And a physician *friend*: what could be better? . . . A physician friend is an automatic guarantee that if, God forbid, you actually get *sick,* you'll get much better, more attentive, more personal care. And it could cost you less, too.

But more than anything, Adult Children of Jewish Parents love *going* to doctors. Why, without the dedicated and faithful patronage of ACoJPs, there would be so very many fewer

- gynecologists
- obstetricians
- pediatricians
- allergists
- internists
- dermatologists
- orthodontists
- psychotherapists
- psychiatrists
- psychics
- nutritionists
- chiropractors
- physical therapists
- acupuncturists
- periodontists
- cosmetic surgeons
- neurologists
- urologists
- gerontologists

You Should Live and Be Well
A Short Guide to Specialty Diseases of Adult Children of Jewish Parents

Colitis

Crohn's Disease

Epstein-Barr

Hypertension

Asthma

Hypoglycemia

Shingles

Herpes

Depression

Diabetes

Urinary Tract Infections

Yeast Infections

Constipation

Anorexia

Bulimia

Arthritis

Dermatitis

Hangnails

Allergies to

cats

dust

mold

yeast

ragweed

goldenrod

nuts

dairy products

nail polish remover

inexpensive makeup

bee and wasp stings

paying full retail price

taking public
transportation

sulfites

cheap wine

For an Adult Child of Jewish Parents, no complaint is too small for a checkup. . . . If, for example, an ACoJP's hair seems to be thinning, it's off to the dermatologist, where diagnostic procedures will certainly include bloodwork—as well as collecting, for at least a week, each and every hair that is left in the ACoJP's hairbrush or comb or that collects in the special trap that will be newly installed in the bathtub drain.

Or, God forbid, there are a few headaches. . . . At minimum, the ACoJP will enthusiastically subject him- or herself to a

CAT scan. All the better if the sulfa imaging drugs used set off a bit of wheezing. Why, that could provide a conversational gambit for months to come. And, of course, there is always a nice headache clinic, like the one at Columbia Presbyterian, or Cedars-Sinai, or the University of Pennsylvania. How pleasant to learn biofeedback from such brilliant young people. How marvelous to be seen by the head of a department. (In the parlance of our people, one calls that being seen by "a very big man.") And then, if one is particularly fortunate, isn't it fascinating to be included in a marvelous new research project—one in which they'll continue to see you, and to call you, for months or years at to come? And let's not forget about all that fine Fiorinal. . . .

And then there's Epstein-Barr disease. Why, even the name is Jewish. This is an excellent disease. Its primary symptom is being particularly tired—which Adult Children of Jewish Parents have been known to become quite often, especially during times of stress. Sometimes one even can have it with few variables that show up on tests. And the cure is just plain wonderful: taking it easy. Epstein-Barr means that the afflicted ACoJP can stay home from work or school on a sustained basis—so often a pleasant plan. And with the right accountant, it might make sustained cruises to the Caribbean tax deductible: a good enough physician friend will prescribe such a trip for your recovery.

ADULT CHILDREN OF
JEWISH PARENTS

Acceptable Behavior	Unacceptable Behavior
collecting antiques	collecting tattoos
driving a Volvo or Mercedes	driving a dune buggy
beating a pillow with a stick	raising your voice to your mother
speaking a bit critically about the dead	not attending funerals
a belief that you are entitled	a belief that you are Princess Anne
blaming your parents	blaming yourself
an urge to return to Italy	an urge to return to Germany
a lust for life	a lust for your son
ecological sensitivity	not flushing the toilet after each use
recycling your seltzer and soda bottles	carrying a big black plastic bag so that you can pick up bottles in the street
a certain need to emulate the rich and famous	a certain need to assassinate the rich and famous
eating to excess	drinking to excess
Halcion	heroin

5. ADULT CHILDREN OF JEWISH PARENTS ENJOY HAVING A FEW NICE THINGS.

The topic one evening at an Adult Children of Jewish Parents meeting was shopping. When I asked them to talk about what shopping meant to them, I heard statements like "I love to shop; it's why I work" and "I am, therefore I shop." When I asked some grown children of Jewish parents to explain further, this is what I heard:

Deanna: *"One story my family tells is that when I was a little girl, my aunt asked me what I wanted for Chanukah— and I said, 'Everything!' I still feel that way."*

Mitchell: *"Not me, not really; I just want antiques."*

Martin: *"I don't get this antiques business . . . I like my stuff new. It gives me the willies to think about someone else I don't even know having eaten from a dish I'm using or a fork or spoon. You know, having put it in their mouth."*

Deanna: *"When I go to sleep at night, I play this game with myself: I've won some kind of contest from American Express. And for the period of a year, I can charge anything I want to it—and I'll never get billed for it. So every night that's how I go to sleep: shopping."*

Mitchell: *"I like Puiforcat silver, and that sort of thing, but what I actually buy is what I guess you'd call 'collectibles.' Right now I'm concentrating on dog planters from the forties, fifties, and sixties. I have 217 of them: poodles, Scotties, terriers, spaniels, pugs. Mostly Scotties. I have them all over my kitchen. I had shelves built for them."*

Martin: *"I like cars: new cars. I just bought an XJ6. A guy I know, a Brit, told me that in England they call that a 'Jewish Rolls-Royce.' "*

Deanna: *"At first, I had no system. I'd go to sleep kind of in a frenzy, because I envisioned myself going from store to store, charging wildly."*

Mitchell: "*I collect a few other things, too: salt and pepper shakers in the shape of furniture and appliances; John F. Kennedy ceramic head banks; tablecloths with covered wagons on them; paint-by-numbers pictures of kittens; plastic figures of Santa Claus from the fifties and sixties; British royal family commemoratives; bowling and golfing trophies; and small taxidermed animals, preferably in glass cases.*"

Martin: "*That's all just junk. . . . What I collect is property. That you can resell. . . . I wait until a piece of luxury property is foreclosed, then I buy it. The recession we're just coming out of ultimately is going to make me* really *rich.*"

Deanna: "*But then I came up with categories of things I needed. Shoes, for example. As I'd be zoning out to sleep, I'd be going from store to store all over the city, buying shoes. Bottega Veneta. Manolo Blahnik. Joan and David. Charles Jourdan. Salvatore Ferragamo.*"

Mitchell: "*Every time I go to a flea market, there's the constant temptation to start another collection. Last week I saw an Elvis plate I almost bought. But can you imagine what would happen if I succumbed to Elvis? Velvet Elvis wall hangings . . . Elvis lamps . . . Elvis clocks . . .*"

Martin: "*Land is the only thing that counts. Land and money.*"

Deanna: "*But shopping for just one item at a time got rather taxing. So instead, I decided to shop specific streets: Fifty-seventh Street in Manhattan, for example, or Madison Avenue, or Fifth. Or I'd change cities. I'd fly to L.A., or Palm Beach, and shop my way down Rodeo Drive or Worth Avenue.*"

Mitchell: "*I don't want to think about buying stuff; I want the actual goods. And lots of them.*"

Martin: "*What I'd like to be is the Donald Trump of the nineties.*"

Deanna: *"Lately, though, as I go to sleep I shop the world. I fly to Paris and do some shopping there. Or I systematically work my way across the Ponte Vecchio. All those antique cameos . . . all those Deco diamond bracelets with rubies. . . ."*

Mitchell: *"Sometimes I do wonder if I'll ever reach the point when I won't want to go to antique shows and flea markets anymore, what I'll do then. I can't imagine what I would do with myself. Or I wonder what would happen if one day I woke up and looked around my apartment, at the sheer volume of things in it, and said to myself, That's all, that's enough. . . ."*

Martin: *"That won't happen. It's never enough."*

SERENITY PRAYER
FOR ADULT CHILDREN
OF JEWISH PARENTS

God grant me the serenity
To accept the things I cannot charge,
Courage to charge the things I can,
And the wisdom to know the difference.

The First Nationa
ADULT CHILDREI

THE CONCORD HOTE

"MO-THER...."

For thousands of Adult Children of Jewish Parents, that one word can mark the first tentative step in a life-long journey towards change.

For others it has come to represent a symbol of the courage it has taken to share some of the most *kishke*-grinding moments of healing in the recovery process.

That's why, this year, to celebrate the thousands of Adult Children of Jewish Parents in recovery, and the professionals who have helped them, we will gather joyfully at the Concord Hotel. To

> **M** *ark for ourselves how far we have come;*
>
> **O** *ne step at a time, nurture our new passion for living;*
>
> **T** *hink about our ability to exercise wisdom and choice;*
>
> **H** *eal the hurting child within;*
>
> **E** *mbrace the love of healthy, supportive relationships;* and
>
> **R** *ejoice in our new gift of intimacy.*

A Celebration of Diversity

We come from all regions of the country. We come from all walks of life. We are married. We are single. We are heterosexual. We are gay. Yet what we share, each one of us, is the journey. . . the powerful and blessed journey towards recovery.

Come celebrate with us this June 5 through 7. Come celebrate this renewel of our courage to change.

Convention of ———
F JEWISH PARENTS

iamesha Lake, New York June 5–7

Convention Chairperson
DR. ANNA SEQUOIA
Founder/Director, the Institute for
Adult Children of Jewish Parents

Special Guest Speakers
ELIZABETH TAYLOR
WILDING TODD FISHER
BURTON BURTON WARNER
FORTENSKY
Topic: You are *not* who you marry

JOAN RIVERS
Topic: It's a Dog's Life: Pets and
the Recovery Process

Programs for Counseling Professionals
Tsouris and the Adult Child of
Jewish Parents: A Skills -Oriented
"Clinical Track"(Continuing
Education Units will be awarded)

Adult Children of Jewish Parents in Recovery
(Choice of Two Learning Tracks)
- "Welcome" workshops for
  Newly Recovering ACoJPs
- Massaging the Child Within
  (experimental)

SPECIAL CATERING BY
Chef Wolfgang Puck of
Spago, Beverly Hills,
California and
The Carnegie Deli,
New York City, New York

Special Discount "Early Bird" Fee
Only $895 per person. First- class
accommodations only

**Register Now Before It's Too Late
Call 1-800-TSOURIS**
*(Please have your Amex, MC, or
Visa ready.)* In person registration:
5% discount for cash.

JEWISH PARENT LAW: WHEN TO PHONE HOME

For the purpose of clarity, the word *child* as it is used below refers to anyone who has one or more parents.

What Kind of Day It is	How Often to Call
An ordinary workday, when parent(s)/child live within a sixty-mile radius.	Once is enough. Call from work: it's cheaper.
Weekend.	Twice during the weekend would be nice, but once is okay.
An ordinary workday, when parent(s)/child live in different cities.	Once a day would be nice, from work. But every other day would be fine.
When away on a [domestic] business trip of two days or more.	Every other morning or evening, from the hotel. Charge it to the company.
When returning from a business trip.	Call when you change planes; this will provide a subject of conversation (I'm at Stapleton Airport; yes, they still have that hologram vender)— plus it fills otherwise wasted time while waiting for a plane.
When away on a [domestic] pleasure trip of two days or more.	Every other day, by prearrangement. Let Mother have the number of the hotel where you'll be, plus your flight numbers.
Business and/or pleasure trips to Europe or Asia.	Once every four or five days is fine, if you can hold out that

	long. More often if someone at home is sick. Leave an itinerary in case, God forbid, someone has a heart attack while you're away.
Business and/or pleasure trips to South America or the Middle East (except Israel).	You don't need to go there.
Jewish holidays.	What's the matter, you've become so fancy you can't spend the holidays at home with your family? Assuming you are away doing your residency in cardiology, here are the rules: Wait until you know your family has just sat down to dinner or is having dessert—then call. You will speak, briefly, with all the visiting aunts and cousins—in the process providing the *naches* your parents so well deserve.

The Grandchild Exemption

The above rules are suspended when the child fulfills his or her mission in life and produces one or more grandchild. You will find, at that point, that your Jewish parents no longer manifest the slightest interest in speaking with you—and will speak only with the grandchild. This continues until the grandchild leaves for college, whereupon the above rules go back into effect.

6. ADULT CHILDREN OF JEWISH PARENTS PHONE HOME ON OCCASION.

A properly behaved Adult Child of Jewish Parents will phone home at least once a day, whether there is anything new to report or not. This call is made to allay his or his parents' anxieties—and his or her own. It is a call that provides reassurance: Mom and Dad are still there and still okay; daughter or sonny-boy are doing fine, despite all the dangers.

If only one parent survives, the call becomes even more important: should the Adult Child of Jewish Parents miss even one day, that is the very day his or her mother or dad will fall on the bathroom floor and be lying there, alone, with a broken hip.

Even if both parents are still healthy and lively, a daughter living alone is required by Jewish Parent Law to phone home daily. If she doesn't, or perchance decides not to answer her phone, a friend from across the street will certainly show up at her door, called by her parents to make sure she's not lying dead on *her* floor. Or the police will show up. Or Mom and Dad will make a personal, uninvited appearance. Just in case . . .

The rules change if a son or daughter has moved to another state. Then the call must be made at least three times a week. Anything less than that is a sure sign of an Adult Child of Jewish Parents in rebellion, in conflict—usually, an ACoJP in therapy (certainly, a person who ought to be attending 12 Step meetings of Adult Children of Jewish Parents). Or, as a Jewish mother will phrase it, with a delicate lilt of sarcasm, "She [or He] has no time for me. . . ."

And then there are those who do not call at all—or call and ask to speak with one parent only (most commonly, a son will not speak with his mother and insist upon speaking with his father). The scientific term for this phenomenon is "stabbing your mother in the heart."

7. ADULT CHILDREN OF JEWISH PARENTS BELIEVE THEY MAY NEED A LITTLE IMPROVEMENT.

Although some few Jewish parents cultivate in their children the belief that each is God's gift to the Jewish-American male or female—or to the professions of law, medicine, or business, most have preferred to take quite the opposite tack. If little Barry was exceptionally smart, a "genius," in fact, Momma was sure to remind Barry, on a regular basis, what a klutz he always was. Or if little Renée was exceptionally pretty, but at ten or twelve years old had a normal bit of baby fat left, her father was sure to call her "Sadie Two-by-Four." Or if little Edie was doing well in math, her mother would point out how much better Cousin Maxine was doing in math *and* English.

One might submit that these patterns of comparison making (some might call it abuse) seem to cut across [Jewish] cultural and class lines. It is, we've observed in many clients at the Institute, as common among nontraditional parents as among traditional parents. Republican parents do it as much as Democrats. Virtually no one is exempt.

What's more, as most Adult Children of Jewish Parents can attest, these comparisons do not end when you turn twenty-one. And if Momma isn't here to make them, why, we do it ourselves. We've been well trained that way. Following are comments made by Adult Children of Jewish Parents concerned about this part of their personalities. You may well recognize yourself, in whole or in part.

Michael F., a forty-year-old former commodities trader, told us:

I grew up in Brooklyn, not far from where they filmed Saturday Night Fever. *My dad was a cabdriver—but the whole time I was growing up, he kept telling me about this friend of his from the old neighborhood, who'd gone to Chicago and made a fortune in the commodities exchange there.*

So in the late sixties, when everyone I'd grown up with was listening to Bob Dylan and smoking pot, I dropped out of Brooklyn College, got on a train with three hundred dollars I'd earned working part-time at Abraham and Straus, and wound up on the floor of the Chicago Commodities Exchange, working as a runner.

By the late seventies I had a seat on the New York Stock Exchange, three and a half million dollars, a big house in Westport, Connecticut, a wife, and a son, Georgie. The rug in the living room alone cost me forty-five thousand dollars. Georgie used to run his Tonka trucks over it.

In a day, I could do a trade that would net me tens of thousands of dollars. I'd take my wife, or my wife and some of her friends, to the Palm, or whatever restaurant was hot, and we'd order half the menu. I'd take home whatever was left and get up in the middle of the night and finish it. Then I'd get up in the morning, go to the exchange, and make more money. It was so easy. Except inside, I knew that even if I was being wooed by Salomon Brothers and playing racquetball at the New York Athletic Club with a bunch of fast-track goyim, I was still just fat Mikey from Brooklyn.

So in 1982 I decided to make some changes. I sold my seat on the exchange, put almost a million bucks into a trust for Georgie, had my nose done, some hair transplanted, lost forty pounds, and got a tan. Then I bought a few hundred acres in Colorado, where I started the Ashram of the Children of Abraham, dedicated to a low-technology, nonpolluting, unworldly life-style.

How was I to know that old sleepy Aspen would become such a hot town?

Robbi M., a twenty-nine-year-old painter with two recovering Adult Children of Jewish Parents parents, put it this way:

My parents have always considered themselves liberals. They met in college, when Dad was at Rensselaer and Mom was at Russell Sage. Early on, they decided to move west, to get away from both sets of their parents. First they went up to Wash-

ington State, to Seattle, and then Dad got a job offer in California, in Silicon Valley.

Early on, my mother decided to stay home with me and my brothers. But, of course, she wouldn't want to be just a mother. . . . So she spends part of each day in the ceramic studio Dad set up behind the garage, making menorahs in the shape of little old Jewish men from shtetls. I don't know where she ever got such shtetl-consciousness from. Maybe from reading too much Shalom Aleichem or Isaac Bashevis Singer. She grew up in Sands Point, Long Island, on the water—not exactly an American Vitebsk.

The whole time I was growing up, my parents would tell me how lucky I was to have such liberated, postpsychotherapy parents. They'd tell me how bad their parents were, especially my father's mother. Then they'd insist that I go to temple with them, so we could parade our family unit in front of all the stepfamilies in our congregation. Reform, of course. The kind where the benches look like they were made in Sweden or Denmark, the building itself is as nondenominational-looking as possible, more like walking into the prow of a great boat than walking into a synogogue, and the one big stained-glass window looks like it belongs in a chapel at the UN: stylized Caucasian, Oriental, and black men and women holding hands, their faces looking toward heaven.

And then at dinner my mother would tell me how well all her friends' daughters were doing—and by implication how well I wasn't. Mrs. Katzen's daughter, Dawn, had just gotten a Westinghouse Science Scholarship and a National Merit Scholarship. Leslie Feinberg's daughter, Hope, wasn't just premed, she was engaged to a boy who was also premed. And there I was, "artistic," going to Antioch because I couldn't get into "someplace better."

And now that I just had a piece bought by the L.A. County Museum of Art, is that good enough? Obviously not . . . because as soon as I tell Mother about that, she quickly counters with the news that "Dawn Katzen's mother tells me she's making $140,000 a year on her own. And that doesn't even include what Harvey is bringing in." Just so I don't get a swelled head. . . .

ADULT CHILDREN OF JEWISH PARENTS'
Six Greatest (Non-Health-Related) Fears

- You will have to move back into your parents' home to live.
- Your father will move in with you.
- Your mother will move in with you.
- Your daughter will turn out exactly like your mother.
- Your son will turn out exactly like your mother.
- *You* will turn out exactly like your mother.

---

8. ADULT CHILDREN OF JEWISH PARENTS ARE QUITE SUPPORTIVE OF ONE ANOTHER.

A certain amount of competitiveness is built into the American educational system. Today, most public schools no longer seat elementary school children by rank—the child with the highest grades in seat one, the child with the second highest grades in seat two, and so on—but remnants of that kind of thinking linger, even in expensive private day schools.

In society at large, competitiveness is further encouraged: in sports, in business. In what we own and in the way we look. People compete for academic prizes, for grants, for money, for position, for prosperous or potentially prosperous husbands or trophy wives—and, of course, for flattering exposure in the press.

And to this great stew of competition, the American Jewish family—those not yet in recovery—add a few extra ingredients. Parents encourage competition between brother and sister, or sister and sister, or brother and brother. Sometimes in less than obvious ways and sometimes quite directly, each child is told how much better the other one is or is doing—or how much worse.

In some families cousins are pitted against each other like fighting cocks, by the simple expedient of a few incisive, parental words of comparison. The children of your parents' friends are added to the mix. Even the extended families of parents' friends will be used in this way: "I just don't understand why you're having such trouble finding a job as an economist. Evelyn Moskowitz's nephew—you know, the one who rented the villa in Fiesole last summer for a month and invited her to visit for a week—just got out of graduate school two, three years ago, and he got a job in Geneva, Switzerland, as chief economist for the European Economic Community."

Add to this stew the distinct message that, as an Adult Child of Jewish Parents, you will never be good enough (as delineated in #7, page 67: "Adult Children of Jewish Parents Believe They May Need a Little Improvement")—and the juices of competition will become even more piquant.

Laura D., for example, expressed it this way:

I've always been crazy for animals. I just love them. From the time I was a little girl, I wanted to be a veterinarian. My first real job, after the summer I worked as an assistant counselor at Camp Ramaca, was cleaning the cages for the vet who took care of my cocker spaniel, Oscar.

At the time I went to Cornell vet school, I was one of the few women in the program. And I was one of only two people who, after graduation, decided to open inner-city practices. My clinic is in the South Bronx, and I also work a couple days a week at the Animal Medical Center, in Manhattan, in the oncology department.

All that would be great—I mean it is great, I've achieved exactly what I set out to do with my life. But there are other things I haven't done, like get married, or have children. I have five cats in the house, all of them rescues from the street, but in my family, at least, that doesn't count.

The only one who gets any respect in my family is my cousin Ellen the Cow (not to impugn cows), because right out of college she married Max—an Israeli without a green card, a formal education, or cash. But Uncle Fred set Max up in a tiny discount electronics store—and now Max has parlayed that into more than thirty stores; his is one of the few electronics chains that survived the recession.

Ellen and Max have a son, Danny; houses in Great Neck and Bridgehampton, and condos on Ocean Drive, in Miami Beach, and in Vail. Ellen doesn't work; she spends most of her time shopping. She wears a lot of fur. And her only conversation to me is, "Are you seeing anyone?" It's not a question; it's an indictment.

Of course, that I see Max in that blue Cadillac cruising around the South Bronx picking up junkie hookers . . . that doesn't count. It certainly won't stop my mother from calling periodically to report the latest tale about Ellen and Max's most recent acquisition. Or to ask me, in that voice that sounds like it's given up hope, "Do you think I'll ever have any grandchildren to knit for?"

Sometimes, even relationships with our closest friends can be affected. As with Sarah F.:

My friend Patty and I have known each other for almost a dozen years. We met when I was an editorial assistant and she was an assistant in the publicity department at a book publishing house. We hit it off right away. We had similar senses of humor, and made each other laugh all the time. We spent a lot of time together, getting ourselves invited to parties for authors, and to gallery openings. We had a lot of fun.

Professionally, we were always helpful to each other, too. After I became a book packager, she turned me on to several people with interesting ideas that needed developing. And when I had something I knew was going to do well, I'd always tell her about it, so she could have a shot at bringing it in to whichever house she was working at at the time.

And then I had an idea for a book project I decided to write myself. It did great, it sold almost three hundred thousand copies in trade paper. I was on a lot of talk shows. And I couldn't help but notice that my good friend Patty was sud-

denly too busy to have lunch with me anymore. Or I'd call her, and she'd sound distant, preoccupied. So we never had a fight or anything, but after a while we essentially stopped seeing each other.

And then I ran into her on the street recently, and I said to her, "Tell me . . . tell me what happened. Why did you stop being my friend?" And she said to me, "Oh, I didn't stop being your friend. I've just been very busy. Jackie O. is writing a blow-by-blow account of her marriage to Ari, and I'm helping her with it."

Be that as it may, when it comes to competitive feelings, it's probably brothers and sisters (or sisters) who take the prize. Sheryle L. expressed it rather tellingly in this poem:

> *Squalling red face,*
> *Tiny hands clasping in time to*
> *piercing wails.*
> *Blue plastic ducks that dance*
> *in time to baby's milky screams.*
> *I said, when they asked,*
> *that I wanted a horse,*
> > *not a brother.*
> > *NOT A BROTHER!*
> *I meant it.*

9. ADULT CHILDREN OF JEWISH PARENTS HAVE HIGHLY DEVELOPED COMMUNICATION SKILLS.

When Grandmother and Grandfather, or Great-grandmother or Great-grandfather, emigrated to this country, chances are there were some relatives they never saw again. Not by necessity: by choice. For one of the fine traditions our forebears brought from the old country was the intrafamilial feud.

Think back. Try to remember, if you can, stories about a Tante This or Tante That. Someone nobody talked to for years. Or consider your father's family or your mother's. Surely, when you mull over the matter, you will recall at least one uncle who suddenly stopped speaking to another. Or a mother-in-law and a daughter-in-law who had a falling-out. Or perhaps in your family it's a series of cousins who don't speak. Or first cousins who've never even met.

Laura G., at a recent series of inner yenta workshops held at the institute, spoke for many of us when she voiced her thoughts. Perhaps you'll find significant echoes of your family life as well.

I don't know if my family is typical. Apparently Grandpa Harry, my father's father, was one of seven brothers, all of whom came to this country as very young men. Right off the bat—or should I say right off the boat—Grandpa Harry had virtually nothing to do with five of the brothers, so I probably have lots of first cousins on that side I've never met, and God knows how many second cousins.

Then there's Uncle Joe and Uncle Sammy, my father's older brothers. They were in business together, as attorneys, but they had a disagreement. So when they dissolved their partnership, Uncle Sammy stopped talking to Uncle Joe, and he forbade Aunt Carol to talk to Aunt Louise, and that's the way it stayed until Uncle Sammy died of an unexpected heart attack.

As for the cousins, Cousin Eddie (the son of Uncle Cornelius, who was Sammy and Joe's and my father's younger brother) hardly ever spoke to any of us after he married that girl from Goucher and moved to Baltimore. As my mother put it, "He got fancy." He has two daughters I've seen only two or three times in my life.

As for my cousins Sharon and Marsha Lynn, Sammy's daughters, we have nothing to do with each other because, well, we were pitted against each other from the time we were kids.

On my mother's side, there's my grandmother's sister, Aunt Masheh. My grandmother, Golda, lived right across the street from Masheh for thirty years, and for more than twenty-five years of that time they never spoke to each other.

Then there's Gus, my mother's older brother. No one in the family ever talked to the woman my uncle Gus married, because she wasn't Jewish. That was in the late thirties, early forties, and that kind of thing wasn't done. But that marriage didn't last.

Today, the only one on my mother's side who doesn't speak to anyone is my cousin Lee. I don't know what that was about. But she has three children I've never met, whom her sister, Debbie, saw a couple times and refers to as "the no-neck monsters."

And of course I'm not talking to my brother and sister-in-law right now. Aside from that, we all get along fine. . . .

10. ADULT CHILDREN OF JEWISH PARENTS HAVE A DEEP SENSE OF COMMUNITY AND CIVIC AWARENESS.

Most Adult children of Jewish Parents are raised with the conviction that the world is divided into two types of people: Jewish people and non-Jewish people. *Us.* And *Them.*

Although some non-Jewish people are Italian—which means they might as well *be* Jewish people—they are still, technically, not Jewish people. They are, technically, *Them.* But not really. Especially when Angie and Joe, for example, both Italian people, are your parents' best friends.

It's only when you begin to date that Angie and Joe's family will suddenly become *Them*—and off limits, no matter how attractive their children might be. After all, you are to date *Us*—not *Them.* And when the time comes to marry, well, there is no choice. One is to marry one of *Us.*

Given their *penchant* for rebellion—and a certain naive belief that non-Jewish men and/or women have fewer irritating foibles—it is no wonder then that so many Adult Children of

Jewish Parents both date and marry *Them*. A recent study sponsored by the Institute for Adult Children of Jewish Parents reveals that 77.3 percent of all institute clients and workshop participants have dated *Them*. Fully 68.4 percent have participated in consensual coitus with *Them*. And 53.6 percent have married *Them*. In 1990, the most recent year for which information was available, approximately 42.4 percent of second marriages were to *Them*.

For years, as we all know, the nonintermarriage code was strictly enforced. Any one of *Us* who married any one of *Them* was struck from the family. And this process often went beyond simply not receiving a Rosh Hashanah card or not being invited to seders. Parents were known to sit *shiva* for children "lost" to them by intermarriage.

But what was all the fuss *really* about? As a therapist who has spent an entire career working with Adult Children of Jewish Parents—and the parents who love them—I can tell you in one word what the crux of the problem is:

Grandchildren

Jewish parents do not want to hear about "hybrid vigor." They want grandchildren who do not go to church.

But will they reject a grandchild who goes to Grace Church School? Of course not. First, their hearts will break. Then they will pick themselves up—and head straight for Toys "Я" Us.

MOTHER'S RULES
FOR MARRIAGE

1. He should make a living.

2. He should be Jewish.

3. He shouldn't drink, gamble, or run around with other women.

4. He should bathe regularly.

5. He shouldn't be so old that he needs to use a walker.

6. He shouldn't hit.

7. Preferably both of his parents should have passed away.

8. He should come to dinner.

MOTHER'S RULES FOR A
SECOND MARRIAGE

1. He should have a few dollars.

2. He should be alive.

MOTHER'S REVISED RULES
FOR A SECOND MARRIAGE

1. He should be alive.

MORE MOTHER'S RULES:
Eleven Perfectly Good Reasons You Wouldn't Want to Marry a Non-Jewish Person

1. They serve such small portions.

2. Who would understand your acerbic comments?

3. What can they get for you wholesale?

4. What if I die? Who will make potato latkes for you then?

5. At Christmas, you'll get one big gift, instead of eight different gifts for Chanukah.

6. They think Lender's makes a great bagel.

7. They hardly ever know a really good caterer.

8. When they get angry, what if they use the word "Jewish" in a pejorative way?

9. At Pesach, will they surprise you with a nice matzoh brie? (If you think that's pronounced "bree," you already have a problem.)

10. How do you think it would make your father feel? God forbid, he could have a heart attack. . . .

11. You would break your mother's heart.

Jeffrey B., a cardiologist—one of the dozens of physicians who have found their way, as clients, to the Institute for Adult Children of Jewish Parents—explains it this way:

I grew up just outside Baltimore, in an observant family. I was a chedar-buchar, *and I was always a good boy: I got great grades, I won a scholarship to Brandeis, and in my second year of medical school, I married a nice, Reform Jewish girl from Cleveland, a performance artist.*

When I found out that her performance art consisted of her sitting in a booth behind a glass window in a Times Square strip joint, charging seventy-five cents a peek, we got an annulment.

My family went nuts from that, and of course I went into analysis. But everybody calmed down when I met Chana. Chana was the girl, everyone agreed, I should have married in the first place. She was very religious. When we married, Chana shaved her long hair off. And she was a real baleboosteh: Chana cooked, she cleaned, and she kept kosher.

Chana and my mother understood each other perfectly. I should have known that was a bad sign. They spoke on the phone twice a day. They laughed, they made plans. And they shopped: first, my mother bought Chana some bright white cotton brassieres—the kind with three-inch backs, and incredibly wide straps—and Chana enthusiastically wore them. Then my mother bought Chana some ankle-length flannel nightgowns—and Chana gladly put those on. And then one day I came home from the hospital early—and I found the two of them at a bridge table in the living room, setting up mah-jongg tiles. Each had pink plastic curlers in her short hair, partly covered by an unpressed shmatte tied at the nape of the neck. Each wore a wrinkled, sleeveless, floral cotton muumuu, old slippers, and diamond stud earrings. And suddenly it hit me, what I had done: I had married my mother.

Needless to say, Chana cleaned me out financially. . . .

And then six and a half years ago, I walked into the ER at Mount Sinai—a patient of mine had been taken there with a heart attack—and I met Felicia. She's a nurse. She's young. She's gorgeous. She has a fabulous body. And she's African-American. We've been living together almost since the day we met. This is a woman who has never heard of flannel nightgowns. I'm passionately in love with her, and I want to have a child with her; she'll be thirty-one this year, so she'd still be young enough. But Felicia wants to get married.

The question is, if I marry Felicia, and my mother does die of a broken heart, how will I be able to live with myself then?

11. Adult Children of Jewish Parents Are Relaxed and Casual in Their Relationships with Others.

Picture this: One day you are working at home, peacefully sitting on your most comfortable chair, plucking a chicken. Suddenly you hear the sound of horses' hooves hitting the packed earthen road outside. They stop. You hear voices. They are speaking Russo-Polish (not a pretty sound). The door bursts open and . . . they're looking for your husband, or your son, to send them to freeze to death in the czar's army. Or they want all your money. Or they want you to move. Or they'd simply noticed how appealingly buxom you or your daughter are, and they've come, shall we say, courting.

Or contemplate another scenario: Your husband, Schlomo, and you have been married eight years and have four surviving children. One day the children are all either napping or playing outside, and you're peacefully sitting down on your most comfortable wooden chair, resting your legs on the bench opposite you, to help with the edema. Suddenly the door bursts open and . . . it's Schlomo. His face is all flushed. He hands you a paper, fills a box with a few of his things, and leaves. You never hear from him again. He sends no money. You've been divorced.

It's no wonder, then, that when our forebears came to this country, they decided that in America, things would be different. And they did their very best to make that happen. In fact, that is how Adult Children of Jewish Parents came to believe in one of the most basic ACoJP tenets:

Control Can Be Fun.

Of course, despite its totally understandable cultural roots, this behavioral trait has upon occasion been known to cause a certain amount of discord. That's why the topic one recent evening, at an Institute of Adult Children of Jewish Parents workshop, was devoted to this very subject.

Gail: "*My problem's my mom. I wasn't dating enough to suit her, so without even asking my permission, she puts an ad in* New York *magazine, in the Personals. The headline, I found out later, was 'MY BEAUTIFUL, THIN SMART DAUGHTER WHO CAN COOK.'*"

Randi: "*At least she has enough imagination to put 'thin' in the headline. My mother-in-law, on the other hand, has no imagination at all—unless it's scenarios of disaster. Last week we get a frantic call from my sister-in-law, who says she's just spoken to my mother-in-law—and she has to speak with Larry, my husband, immediately. So Larry gets on the phone, all upset, and she tells him that the week before, their father went to the doctor, and the doctor said the old man's blood sugar was sky high. And if the old guy doesn't cut out the bowls of ice cream every night, he will definitely develop diabetes—and drop dead. Larry's father, she says, is still eating ice cream—and Larry should get him on the phone right away, and tell him to stop it.*"

Steve: "*I wouldn't exactly say that my lover, Lewis, and I are having any kind of a problem about control. We're just supposed to go up to the Cape, to Chatham, to visit his old roommate from college, Bob. And Lewis says if I insist upon taking my car, he'll cancel the trip.*"

Gail: "*So all of a sudden I get these wads of letters from men, some photocopied, with my name handwritten into the salutation, some accompanied by photos. One guy actually enclosed a picture of himself naked, with an erection. I thought about sending that photo to my mother; I should have, no? But a few of the letters sounded kind of interesting. . . .*"

Randi: "*So my darling sister-in-law dumps this load of anxiety on my husband—and two seconds later, she takes off for Manhasset Miracle Mile to look for bargains. . . .*"

Steve: "*I really don't see why we couldn't take my car. I just had a rebuilt carburetor installed. So what if the car is a little rusty? All Lewis has to do is watch where he puts his feet.*"

Gail: *"So I did go out with a couple of guys who answered. I met each one in a safe, public place, of course. And now I'm actually going to see one of them, Richard, for a third time. He's an engineer. But last night I found out from my aunt Irene that my mother has hired a private detective to find out if Richard really is who he says he is, to verify whether or not he's married, or been in jail or something—and to check his credit rating and income!"*

Randi: *"This kind of stuff has been going on the whole time I've been married. Of course Larry made the call . . . I told him not to. God forbid the old guy should be left alone to make an adult decision on his own. . . ."*

Steve: *"It's really not that bad-looking a car. It's a 1970 Chrysler Le Baron, so it's nice and big. . . . I've actually moved furniture in that backseat. . . ."*

Gail: *"I'm really grateful to my mom: I've been out of the house for fifteen years now—but she still takes such good care of me. . . ."*

Randi: *"And then last night, late, my sister-in-law calls— she's just talked with her delightful mother—and she wants Larry to get on the phone with his dad again and tell him what not to eat. And I just couldn't take it anymore. So I said to my husband, 'Larry, listen, I would never presume to tell you what to do—especially about your family. But I will say this: If your sister calls here one more time to tell you to tell your dad what he can or cannot eat, I am personally going to bake the gooiest, creamiest, most fattening cake I can think of—and hand-deliver it to your dad along with two gallons of his favorite ice cream. . . ."*

Steve: *"But it's not like I can't compromise. We're going to fly up to Boston, then rent a T-bird. Lewis will just have to pay for it all. . . ."*

MOTHER'S GUIDELINES FOR CHOOSING A PET

1. Is it expensive?

2. Is it attractive?

3. Can you wear it?

---

12. ADULT CHILDREN OF JEWISH PARENTS BELIEVE THAT GUILT HAS TAKEN QUITE A BAD RAP.

Many Adult Children of Jewish Parents believe that you can't be too guilty. This concept has been fed to them with their orange juice.

Take the case of Sue G., for example:

> *Every morning, my mom would squeeze fresh orange juice for me and my brother. She told us it was because we were so special. Then she'd sit down at the table with us and eat the pulp. Every day we'd have the juice—and she'd have the pulp. And every day it used to tear me apart inside, that she was making such sacrifices for us. . . .*
>
> *To this day, if I buy something for myself, I have to justify it. I think what it's about is that if I have something good, it means someone else has to go without. Even when I met Mitchell, my second husband, it was hard to accept that it was okay to have such happiness. It was like, how did I have a right to be so happy, when so many others aren't. . . .*

To give credit where credit is due, what role does Mother (or even Dad) play in the formation of guilt? A great deal, bless her (or his) heart. If Mother was unhappy in her life or marriage, or emotionally, spiritually, or intellectually unfilfilled, she could always be counted upon to pass that information on to us. And the same goes for Dad.

Of course, there *is* a bright side to guilt. Were it not for ACoJP guilt, just think how many hospitals would have only one (old) building. . . .

TWENTY-NINE PERFECTLY LEGITIMATE REASONS
for an Adult Child of Jewish Parents to Experience Guilt

1. You haven't called your mother in the past month.

2. You haven't called your mother in the past week.

3. You haven't called your mother today.

4. You called but right away asked to speak with your father.

5. You're divorced.

6. You're still single.

7. You're gay.

8. You've been indicted for insider trading.

9. You put the S&L or insider trading money in an account where it could be found.

10. You spent money on a cab when you could have taken a bus.

11. You hired a limousine to drive you to the airport.

12. You hired a limousine to drive you to Philadelphia.

13. You spent your parents' retirement nest egg on three pounds of cocaine.

14. You spent your parents' retirement nest egg on three pounds of cocaine that were confiscated by the police.

15. You just paid $135 for 1.4 ounces of Shiseido revitalizing cream.

16. You just paid $400 for a pair of purple suede ankle boots.

17. You just paid $53,000 for a car.

18. You're thinking of going to Paris instead of to the seder.

19. You just ate all the ice cream in the freezer.

20. You just ate all the ice cream in Los Angeles.

21. You've decided to convert to the Episcopal church.

22. You've decided to convert to the Republican party.

23. You haven't produced a single grandchild.

24. You haven't produced a single grandchild, and you're the last of your line.

25. You were in your parents' neighborhood and didn't stop by.

26. You were in your parents' state and you didn't stop by.

27. You just pilfered your mother's last Valium.

28. You've had sex out of wedlock.

29. You've had sex at any time in your life.

PLEASE ADD YOUR OWN

30.

31.

32.

33.

34.

VI

Daddy Dearest: A Quiz

Those of us who have grown up with the phenomenon know that there are at least three types of Jewish dads:

Aaron Spelling

An Aaron Spelling–type father tends to be extremely successful in business or a profession and expects a reasonable amount of deference in the home. When Aaron is home watching TV, or reading the *Times*, he does not rise to get his own glass of seltzer. Mother does it, or one of the children. Luckily, Aaron will do just about *anything* for his children, including put one or more of them on TV.

An Aaron-type dad is also extremely handy when it comes to tuition at expensive schools: he can and will pay. He will also help out after graduation, for as long as it takes you to "settle down" (in some cases you may continue to receive monthly funds through your thirties or forties). He will often provide the down payment for an apartment or a house. And he is, of course, extremely generous to the grandchildren.

All he asks is a little common courtesy: that you call your mother, treat him with respect—and bring the children to visit as often as possible.

Gentle Ben

Gentle Ben may be a teacher or a social worker—or he may work in the Fulton Fish Market. He may have advanced degrees or not. That's not really what he is about: Gentle Ben is the peacemaker. He is an island of calm in a whirlwind of emotion. Your mother may shout or prod or provoke, she may deride or act deranged. Ben's role is to act as the mediator. He keeps a sense of equilibrium in the home. Relatives turn to him when there's trouble, to help sort it out.

Ben will give every last cent he has to his children. All he wants is a little peace in this world—and for them to be happy.

But Ben tends to have rather crazy kids. Perhaps it's because throughout their childhood they've seen Gentle Ben periodically either explode with rage once his long fuse burns down, or they've seen him eaten up by anxiety: calling the police, for example, when he's unable to reach an adult daughter who hasn't mentioned that she'd be away for a weekend.

Sophie Portnoy's Husband

Usually, he's a good-hearted wimp. He may have some worldly success, though often he doesn't; in any case, he knows his place. Women wear the pants in this family. They make the big decisions. They tell him who can be his friends.

As a father, Sophie's husband means well. He may do some "boy stuff" with his son or sons. Generally he has little to do with his daughters.

This type of dad is generous, sometimes beyond his means. Once you produce some grandchildren, you may finally have something to talk about. . . .

Naturally, these three types may overlap—but probably not much. You know which type you have. Now, the time has come to look a little more deeply into your relationship with your father—and find out whether some time spent with an Adult Children of Jewish Parents recovery program might be appropriate. . . .

To proceed, place a check in the box next to the statement or statements that most accurately describe(s) your father or your relationship with your father. Check as many boxes as apply. To calculate your results, see "How to Score," page 90.

[ ] Paid for camp.

[ ] Likes to mix his plaids and stripes.

[ ] Wonders when I'm going to "straighten out and settle down."

[ ] Always loved all my boyfriends (or girlfriends).

[ ] Wears his hair like Sam Donaldson

[ ] Always there with a compliment, like "Want some dessert, fats?"

[ ] Built all those houses in Levittown.

[ ] Might as well be grafted to the TV set.

[ ] Thinks he's Julio Iglesias.

[ ] Chagrined that I'll never join the Jewish War Veterans, or the JWV Ladies' Auxiliary.

[ ] Generally has the *New York Times* in front of his face; could be asleep back there.

[ ] Paid cash for the condo in Palm Beach.

[ ] Rather disappointed with the way I turned out.

[ ] Wishes I'd get married already.

[ ] Exceptionally calm and rational.

[ ] The kind of man who knows his place.

[ ] Always came to open school night.

[ ] Coached my Little League team.

[ ] Is president of the Hair Club for Men.

[ ] Always brought home the groceries.

[ ] Still hates those Japanese.

[ ] Extremely handy around the house.

[ ] A truly happy person.

[ ] A recovering Adult Child of Jewish Parents.

[ ] Proud to be Civil Service.

[ ] Dad? Barely know the guy.

[ ] At least he's not Teddy Kennedy. . . .

How to Calculate Your Score

Give yourself 10 points for every box you checked.
30 points or less—Obviously you are not descended from a Semitic tribe.

40–70 points—Your prognosis is excellent, but sustained attendance at Adult Children of Jewish Parents workshops would be in order.

80 points or more—Without help, you will either become your father or marry your father. Would you want that?

VII

DAILY AFFIRMATIONS FOR ADULT CHILDREN OF JEWISH PARENTS

Recovery is a process. It is an ongoing process that can often be aided by meditation—and by the guided imagery we in recovery circles call affirmations.

Now, as you begin your journey toward recovery, you will discover that affirmations can be very useful along the way. They help us realize who we really are and where, with our Higher Power's help, we can be going. In time you may actually find it is a wonderful thing to awaken a little early each day, so that in the calm and peace of morning you can begin to focus your energy—and savor each day's thoughtful affirmation.

The following pages contain seven days, one full week, of affirmations. Each affirmation has been used by hundreds of clients at the Institute for Adult Children of Jewish Parents and has withstood the tests of resistance and time.

Once you have decided to commit your heart and mind to recovery, you will want to read and contemplate one affirmation each and every day.

Day 1

SUPERVISING THE HELP

Chefs are curiously colour-blind. Leave them to their own devices and you may end up with an all-rose dinner—crème Portugaise, saumon poché with sauce cardinale, jambon with sauce Hongroise, and bombe Marie-Louise.

THE DUCHESS OF WINDSOR

In the process of recovery, we learn to be kinder to the help. We decrease our vigilance and our demands. We accept that punctuality is not always a virtue and that it is normal to want a day off—even if it is a Friday, we're expecting company, and we've had no advance notice. We accept that not everyone understands the importance of using a toothbrush on the bathroom grout. That scratches on the sterling ultimately matter very little. That even Chinese export porcelain can stand a turn or two through the dishwashing machine.

Today, I dare believe in the integrity of the help. Today I trust enough to leave out the garnet pin left to me by Aunt Ida.

Day 2

GROOMING

Mrs. Kennedy would no more see her husband until she fixed her hair and face than Queen Elizabeth would receive the prime minister wearing her bathrobe.

MAUD SHAW

Today I will shake off my resistance and establish new standards of grooming in the home. I will ruthlessly discard all faded sweatshirts and sweatpants. I will replace all sleeping garments not made of silk. With a fearless critical eye, I will assess the state and style of my bathrobes and eliminate any not sexy, flattering, and in pristine condition. I will affirm my worth and goodness by applying a good moisturizer, undereye cover, and at least a little blusher before appearing before my family in the morning—even if I am the single parent of a child or a cat.

Today I let my love shine forth by radiating an attractive and polished appearance. I will begin today by being lovely.

Day 3

COMPULSIVE EATING

No one jumps to personal conclusions about an average size twelve. That is, except people who think average is size six.

WENDY WASSERSTEIN

We used to think that there was joy in a Heath toffee bar, a Baby Ruth, or a Snickers. That there was even more joy in an entire bagful, especially eaten in the course of one evening. We knew that bagels and lox, if just a light shmear of cream cheese was applied, didn't count as far as calories were concerned. And that pizza is the most efficacious cure for the common cold—but only if one consumes three or more slices, with pepperoni and extra cheese.

Today I will concede that Chinese food will not mend a broken heart. That I do not owe my intellect to ice cream. Today I begin a new and rewarding relationship with Brussels sprouts.

Day 4

COMFORT

Never stand when you can sit.

LOUISE SAREZKY

When faced today with the decision of how to best get to my destination, I will take the time to contemplate the possibilities. I will consider all alternative modes of transportation—with an open heart, an open mind, and an open purse. I will try not to listen to people with a taste or need to travel tourist. I will not listen to people who insist upon taking only one suitcase. Rather, I will allow myself to follow my most basic inner needs: to stretch my arms and legs and my lovely, reasonably slim body; to be served decent French champagne; and to place myself within a decor flattering to my skin.

Today I trust my instincts. Today I trust my decision to book on the Concorde to France. Today I have the faith to know that comfort rarely comes cheap.

Day 5

BEAUTY

Every day one's face presents new problems.

IRA VON FURSTENBERG

It is time to take responsibility for the state of our skin. Whatever happened to us in the past, the grime, the sun, the lack of restful sleep—even the inappropriate consumption of Devil Dogs and Ring Dings—is now memory, beyond our control. We can do nothing about it.

What we can do is let go of any blame that we might have for ourselves and our past life-style. We must prepare ourselves to pay a high price for competent beauty advice and for nourishing creams and oils. And be ready, now and all through our future, to undergo any of the discomfort or pain it may take to remain beautiful.

Today I will refill my prescription for Retin-A. I will assure myself that sometime soon the itching and redness and flaky skin will pass. Today I will begin saving in earnest, so that next year I can at least have my eyes done.

Day 6

FAULT FINDING

Criticism—a big bite out of someone's back.

ELIA KAZAN

With our relentless eye for perfection, it is difficult to look at the people around us, even those few we love, with calm, and acceptance, and forgiveness. We tend to see the moles that no one else sees, the little pulled threads, the chip at the edge of the beautiful glass.

> *Today I will overlook the fact that my best friend's dark roots are showing, even though she claims she's a natural blonde. When my newest sweetheart brings me roses, I will not dwell on the slight wilt and darkened edge of some outer petals. And when he or she asks if I am happy, I will not admit (at least I will try not to)—how much better my last friend, the rock star, was in bed.*

Day 7

JEWELRY

I'm one of those unfortunate women who had to buy their own emeralds.

KATHERINE ANNE PORTER

Stop and find a few moments alone today to contemplate your gemstones. Bring your attention to any prong that may need tightening, any clasp that may need repair. With your softest toothbrush and a little warm water (close the drain first), polish away any soil or lotion that may have dimmed their luster.

Study your stones. Their colors are the colors of the best things in life: red for a passion that never fades; green for vitality, renewal; blue for vacations in the Caribbean. And the clear beauty of diamonds—so too sparkles the snow on the slopes of Vail between Christmas and New Year. Diamonds, however, will never melt.

Today I will be grateful for any gem I own, even if it is a small one. I will go to the safe-deposit box today, and be daring, and wear the stones that lie there in the dark. Today I will sparkle from every facet of my being.

VIII

BREAKING THE CYCLE:
The Chutzpah to Change

MOTTO FOR ADULT CHILDREN OF JEWISH PARENTS IN RECOVERY

Let go and let Mother

---

t's not easy to change old conditioning or previous patterns of thought. But it *can* be done—even by Adult Children of Jewish Parents.

On the pages that follow you will discover a number of projects and workshops adapted from recovery methods successfully in use at the Institute for Adult Children of Jewish Parents. Each addresses a specific ACoJP problem. Most can be done at home, either alone or with a friend.

As you begin your recovery process, keep in mind that you don't have to do every workshop exercise the first week. Try not to overwhelm your inner child.

1. ADULT CHILDREN OF JEWISH PARENTS ARE CAUTIOUS: THE CURE

ACoJP Disaster-Anticipation Workshops

These workshops are perhaps best attended in person—but there are many elements you can adapt for home use, either on your own, with a companion, or with your entire family. Perhaps the single most important exercise is

The Single Random Day of Disaster Scrapbook Project. First, purchase a large scrapbook with plain pages. You do not necessarily need an embossed leather cover, but if you find that that aids you in your concentration or willingness to do the project, by all means charge one. Next, go to your local newsstand, where you'll probably have to pay cash, and buy as many local, regional, or national newspapers as you can find. You may include weekly newspapers and news magazines, but not the *Star,* the *Globe,* or the *National Enquirer,* as the inclusion of any one of these may ultimately make you question the validity of this exercise. You may, if you wish, go to a newsstand that carries out-of-town newspapers, in order to get a more national perspective.

Now, systematically go through each newspaper, checking for essentially random, untoward events. Cut out each and every relevant article and paste it in your scrapbook. Here, for example, is just a sampling from one single random day of disaster:

An Unwelcome Guest at Vacation Site

Violent Deaths Disturb the Peace of Mind at Sunny Florida Spot

4★

TOWERING INFERNO IN TIMES SQ.

70 feared dead in China explosions

men
be

stairways to the street.

Fire officials said the two-alarm blaze started at 3 p.m. on the unoccu- floor, where and filing red.

City prepares for worst

Denver's pope plan thing, includ

ners seem to have thought of every-
rst.

KANSAS

PAOLA — Linda Witt will serve 15 years to life for killing her husband, Donald Witt, 7½ hours after they were married for the second time. Witt was asleep when she shot him with the gun she gave him as a wedding present.... Mary Ann Walsh.

World Youth Day participants may igh-altitude heat. Thousands may g the huge Mass Aug. 15. d a transport plane will be stand- tal set up across the street. Casu- to local hospitals and to other eds fill.

Desert Storm," says World Youth "I think they're forgetting

eli-

ays
supposed
area ... It oblem because lot of material

Calif. camp counselor saves boy from rampaging bear

G BEAR LAKE, Calif.
) — A 13-year-old boy g in a sleeping bag nearly scalped by a aging black bear be- eing saved by his counselor.

elor Njal Hansen he 6-foot-tall bear n carried Joshua to safety after attack in the ardino National

ed my life. I would have d into bear

droppings," said the Ojai, Calif., teen, who obviously hadn't lost his sense of humor.

The boy, his head still wrapped with a turban of bandages, spoke to report- ers from his bed at Bear Valley Community Hospi- tal, where he received 150 stitches and underwent two hours of surgery. Doc- tors said part of his scalp was ripped off.

At about 5 a.m. Tuesday, as Joshua slept, "I ... felt something on my chest. I thought it was a raccoon," he said. "I could feel the teeth poking my head and sinking in."

The bear "might have been sick or something, so it's not completely his fault," he added. "But he shouldn't be going around eating kids just because he's sick."

OBITUARIES

Two Eminent Biologists Die in Crash

E
K

ma
"p

Teenager Tearfully Recoun
Learning About Birth Mixup

SARASOTA, Fla.—A teenager
vorce" her biological pare
stand yesterday
learned

AROU

ants to "di
e witness
ment she
her baby th

our on
ire to i of the
1 Re ays Kris
emergency

ng y.
rt. may ham-
t st Sunday or
areas will get
le areas could
s Weather Ser-
Carbone.
Rocher, Ill., the
llowed the his-
omitable resi-
a little easier

puter s
matics
Inte
access
infor
about
from
forest
news
tica."
Asian
even
can b
La
ampl
sever
Inter
versi
trans
play

Hymans Had Enjoyed Wealth and Respect

Business Success Preceded Personal Tragedy

A
b

crash
were not immed
Details of the crash a
come available until Wednesday
night, when Mr. Parker's fiancee
Jacqueline Goerck, who suffered
broken ankle, limped five hou
through densely forested mountai
before making her way on horst

School officials eventually pos
signs that such actions violated the
sexual ha
stopped.

Because
ment body
net, any ki
e by in
me

glasses to fit our personalities,"
Krebs said.
"He certainly seemed to kn
stuff. He was very d
tremely on

ture
sor
led
dep
hur
wo

Left Woman Destitute

Theft of $20,000 From 92-Year-Old

e evidence
d his

Dubester said Lee was transferred to a
Mount Pleasant nursing home in April 1987
and that Lockridge signed an acknowledge-
ent of financial responsibility for her. Nev-
ess, he said, Lockridge never turned
$2,000 monthly ome to the
me

Sewage plants over capacity

The plaintiffs, a coalition of community groups headed by the Coalition for
a Livable West Side, will now ask the
judge to impose a moratorium on new
sewage hookups that would include
Manhattan and delay proposed projects
ch as Donald Trump's Riverside
uth.

The city and the DEC and the fed-
ernment have known for years
th plants are operating in viola-
their permit yet no effecti
s or remedies have b

posed," said John Van Der Tuin, the
attorney for the community groups.
The city Department of Environmen-
tal Protection has been working wi
the DEC under a consent agree
reduce sewage flow into
largely though enco
servation. The
expand the
Ian

crisis," says
olph County
rman. "But
ur guard."
by French
250 years
evees hold.
rishly the
save the
ersial tac-
evee

POSTAL VIOLENCE: U.S. P
next year will undergo wider b
violence in post offices. Postm
Congress. Since 1983, p
eople and wounded 20.
d from 1980 to 1989 was
0.63 postal worker deaths
s compared with 0.71 in pr
or Lee
ridge re-
for $250.
ted Ward 8

a ba
the wat

Howlett
berg

As you can see, a little concern is not entirely out of line. You may, of course, expand the project to become the "Single Random Week of Disaster Project."

Now, you may be saying to yourself, Hey, this is recovery? Looking at all these random disasters is just making me as paranoid as my mother!

What can I tell you? The fact is, like it or not, sometimes your mother is right. Which is why you may also want to try

The Week of Mayo Health and Science Project. For this exercise you will need two clean, dry, empty small glass jars, small ones. Two of the pretty little Crabtree & Evelyn jam jars you've squirreled away, just in case you ever decide to make your own preserves again, would be just right—but even two empty Polaner All Fruit jam jars will do. Now, into each jar measure out one-half cup of mayonnaise. One jar should contain normal commercial mayonnaise and the other "light" mayo. Carefully spoon the mayo into the jars, cover, label each, and place them in a safe, dry place in your kitchen where they will not be disturbed. Avoid windowsills, as this could prejudice the results.

Taking a fresh tablet of paper, which should be used for no other purpose, note the day and time your experiment began. Each day over the course of the next week, carefully observe the changes in the look of the contents of the jars, and take notes. Try to make your observations at the same time each day. For example:

Regular Mayo

Day 1: Attractive, appealing fresh cream color. Virtually cries out for a little tuna and tomato.

Day 2: Somewhat liquefied, appealing fresh cream color. Edges have barest hint of slightly yellow cast.

Day 3: Definite orange cast along the top.

Day 4: Slightly stronger orange cast over top. Beads of clear liquid emerging from top of mayonnaise.

Day 5: Pervasive orange cast. Now it looks more like deli mayonnaise.

Day 6: Outer coating has a deep, translucent orange glaze.

Day 7: Outer coating has a deep, translucent orange glaze, with clear liquid drops emerging from surface.

"Light" Mayo

Day 1: Attractive, appealing fresh cream color. Virtually cries out for a little tuna and tomato.

Day 2: Attractive, appealing, fresh cream color. Virtually cries out for a little tuna and tomato.

Day 3: Attractive, appealing, fresh cream color. Virtually cries out for a little tuna and tomato.

Day 4: Attractive, appealing fresh cream color. Virtually cries out for a little shrimp salad.

Day 5: Edges have barest hint of slightly yellow cast.

Day 6: Edges have barest hint of slightly yellow cast.

Day 7: Edges have barest hint of slightly yellow glaze— nothing that anyone would notice.

Of course, your results may vary slightly. Just keep in mind that mayonnaise used on the food at your local deli or salad bar may be stored very much as ours was during this experiment. They take it out of the refrigerator in the morning and let it stand out all day long, day after day. Maybe they'll cover it and put it back in the refrigerator overnight. But the next day, out it comes again. And again. And again. The only difference in *our* experiment is that we've speeded up the process a bit by not cooling down the bacterial growth at night.

And isn't it interesting that you can eventually *see* the spoilage of regular mayonnaise—but that "light" stuff, why, you could be enjoying a perfectly nice-looking tuna salad and not even know you were gambling with your life.

Now, aren't you hungry for something nice with mayo? And will you ever ignore your mother's advice about mayo again? Of course not.

Furthermore, will you ever bother with "light" mayonnaise again? Not if you're in your right mind, you won't. Why, botulism it could give you—and it doesn't even taste good!

2. ADULT CHILDREN OF JEWISH PARENTS ALWAYS LOOK ON THE BRIGHT SIDE: THE CURE

A bleak worldview is, at best, an inconvenience. Especially when it is not based on actual reality. Which is why you may want to participate in some simple

ACoJP Pragmatism Training

On an 8½-by-11-inch piece of paper, either lined or unlined, make two corresponding lists. On the left, write the headline "What I Like/What I Like to Do." And on the right, write "What Can Happen as a Result."

Now, giving yourself at least ten minutes of uninterrupted time, fill the left-hand column. Include things you like to do, plus things you like to eat. You should have at least ten items in the left-hand column, although with just a little work you could add considerably more.

Next, devoting at least ten to fifteen uninterrupted minutes to the task, write down the possible potential consequences of any item on the left, both good and bad.

You may consult the sample list that follows, recently completed by a recovering Adult Child of Jewish Parents.

What I Like/ What I Like to Do	What Can Happen as a Result
Sitting in the sun	A beautiful, flattering tan; heat exhaustion; premature aging; skin cancer
Walking	A sense of freedom; foot blisters; corns; bunions; overuse of charge cards; (God forbid) a mugging
Running	Weight loss; heat stroke; chafing; dehydration; athlete's foot; nail fungus; fatal heart attack
Sex	A few moments of pleasure; herpes, chlamydia; gonorrhea; genital warts; syphilis; (God forbid) **HIV** infection
Ice cream	A few moments of pleasure; shockingly expensive periodontal problems; diabetes; stroke; fatal heart attack; Hadassah arms
Potato chips	A few moments of pleasure; pouches under eyes; swollen ankles; jiggly thigh expansion; raised cholesterol; untoward weight gain
N.Y. strip steak	A few moments of pleasure; gout; stroke; fatal heart attack
Driving car	Getting from place to place on your own schedule; whiplash; permanent back injuries; cuts and abrasions; paralysis; death
Travel by airplane	Getting from place to place that might be too far to drive; food poisoning; "sick airplane

| | syndrome"; death by trauma and fire |
| Playing with dog or cat | Interspecies affection; allergies; asthma; ticks (Lyme disease); cat scratch disease; schmutz |

Or, to quote Gilda Radner, who was right: It *is* always somethin'. . . .

3. ADULT CHILDREN OF JEWISH PARENTS LIKE A NICE SNACK: THE CURE

As we saw previously, a desire to eat when anxious is one of the determining characteristics of the Adult Child of Jewish Parents. And since Adult Children of Jewish Parents tend to deal with more anxiety than most, snacking (let's call it, to be polite) is one of an ACoJP's primary activities.

Since most ACoJPs who attend institute workshops and 12 Step recovery groups have already experienced—and for a while succeeded and then failed at—virtually every diet plan ever promulgated, we strongly recommend the following recovery program. It is aimed at *total recovery,* once and for all. Unfortunately this is one you cannot do by yourself, without professional guidance. But it does work. It's called

Mother's Fried Herring and Potato Latke Workshop

The most difficult part of the fried herring workshop/cure may well be booking your appointment. Given that ACoJPs travel from both coasts for this cure, and occasionally from as far away as Israel, reservations can be hard to come by. But they are well worth the effort.

Unlike other ACoJP activities and workshops, which are offered in fashionable locations across the country, you will find that Mother's Fried Herring and Potato Latke Workshop is held, at the moment, only in the Bronx and Brooklyn, New York.* This is part of the dynamic of the cure.

Let's look now at how Mother's Fried Herring and Potato Latke Workshop/Cure works. We'll concentrate on the dynamic of our Bronx facility, as this was where the cure was pioneered.

Approved clients line up at Twenty-sixth Street and Madison Avenue, in Manhattan, with exact change for the express bus to the Bronx. Driving there yourself is not allowed, taxicabs to the Bronx are not permitted, limousines are forbidden—and travel there via subway is out of the question.

No reading is allowed during the fifty-minute trip. This is to allow you to concentrate on the contents of the shop windows along Madison Avenue—and then witness the shock of transition as the bus travels through what is generally known as a "rougher neighborhood," as it wends its way toward the Third Avenue Bridge and into the Bronx. Here, one is to concentrate on the state of the Grand Concourse and note how the farther north one goes, the more "normal" it seems. This is part of your transition process—and your lasting cure.

At Bedford Park Boulevard you will be met by your assigned "Daddy"—a pleasant, balding man with a bit of a paunch—who will drive you the remaining five blocks to the appropriate prewar co-op. After parking in the garage, ascending in the attractive wood-paneled elevator, Daddy will ring the apartment bell twice and announce, "Adele, she's [he's] here!" Whereupon Adele, your own "mom for a day," will beam at you as she stands in the doorway of the kitchen, a fluorescent glow lighting her bouffant blond hair like a halo, a wooden spoon in her hand. Adele will come toward you in welcome, press you toward her great polyester-sheathed bosom, and enfold you in her arms.

You will sit down on the plastic-covered couch and begin your snacking. For, the very moment your assigned mother breaks from your first hug, she will ask, "Are you hungry?" And no matter what, the day's parade of food will begin.

On the cocktail table in front of you, Mother will place small

*A third location, on New York's Lower East Side, next to the restored Eldridge Street Synogogue, will be offered sometime next spring (for more information, dial 1-800-TSOURIS). A fourth location, for travelers and/or European ACoJPs, will be opened the following fall in Venice's Ghetto Vecchio.

(but not *too* small), fancy cut-crystal dishes of *mandelbrodt; hamentashen;* egg salad with anchovies; herring with cream sauce; lox and cream cheese on miniature bagels; chopped chicken liver; crackers of various types; M&M's; miniature cannoli; halvah; and a variety of nuts. An ample supply of chilled Dr. Brown's Cel-Ray tonic, in the bottle, is also supplied.

"Have a little something," Daddy will urge as he settles back before the TV, which will remain on during the entire duration of your cure.

For the first hour Mother will remain in the kitchen, while you sit in the living room with Daddy. You do not have to speak with him. Travel magazines will be provided, in case you don't feel like watching the hazy rerun of Victor Mature, in fur loincloth, running from the volcano. Your only obligation is to take a taste of everything on the cocktail table and to polish off at least five dessert dishes full of delicacies. If you wish, you may then retire to the spare bedroom for a twenty-minute nap.

When you emerge, your luncheon will be served. This will consist of salt herring, which has been soaked in cold water and milk for at least twenty-four hours, dredged in flour, pepper, and paprika, and pan-fried with sliced onion in a generous amount of butter. The accompanying dish is potato latkes, hand-grated with onion, mixed with a little matzoh meal, a couple of eggs, a dash of pepper, and pan-fried in rendered chicken fat. Homemade applesauce and warm challah accent the meal.

Mother will sit at the Formica table with you, although she will just pick.

As you dine, Mother will ask, if you are single, if you are seeing anyone. If you are married and have no children, she will ask when she can expect to have the opportunity to start knitting. If you are married with children, she will ask specific questions about the state of your finances, which you are obligated to answer as you eat. You must eat at least six halves of herring and seven large latkes. This is the minimum. An ample supply of seltzer, in the old-fashioned nozzle bottle, will be supplied.

After lunch you may lie down in the spare bedroom for ten minutes.

It is then time for coffee and cake. You will be provided with a strip of apple raisin strudel, a New York–style cheesecake with cherry topping, and a chocolate mousse cake baked just for you by Mary Bender. You will consume at least one sizable slice of each, preferably more.

As you move to the couch, Daddy will get up from his chair and offer you a Cherry Heering, which you must accept. If you wish, he can pour it for you over a little ice cream.

Then Mother will sit down on the couch on one side of you, Daddy will sit on the other, and they will go through the photograph album with you. The photograph album will have your name on the outside, in large gold letters; when Mother opens it up, you will notice that the people inside are all exceptionally large in size. This is the family album of the big people. Barely anyone weighs less than 230 pounds. And Mother will begin: "On this page is your Uncle Alter. That's Aunt Minnie with him, over there. You look quite a bit like her, dear."

Then Daddy will pitch in: "And on this page, why, here's Cousin Beth. Must have been taken before she gained all that weight."

Mother will get quite delighted: "Oh, here, here, look . . . here's Aunt Bessie; you're named for her. Look how much you resemble her now! You could have been twins!" Except the person in the photograph must weigh at least three hundred pounds; she's sitting on a blanket on the beach, wearing a bathing suit. She has huge upper arms like hams, and folds in her thighs. She has big, round shoulders and no neck.

This process will continue throughout most of the entire large album. Except, suddenly, *your* face will start to appear. Clearly, as you'll figure out, it must have been cut from the Polaroids you had to submit the week before your cure—except that your face will have been pasted on top of huge, big, fat people bodies. "And look, dear," Adele, your Mother, will say proudly, turning the pages, "here's you . . . and you . . . and you . . . and you . . ." Then Mother will calmly turn to you and say, "Why don't you stay for dinner, dear? We're having brisket, a nice noodle kugel, kishke, canned peas and carrots—and tzimmes. . . ."

Because of your heightened state of sensitivity and awareness, a limousine will naturally be provided to take you back to

Manhattan. (Clients do tend to return to the city in stunned silence.) An insulated bag of leftover herring and latkes will be provided as you leave the car.

4. ADULT CHILDREN OF JEWISH PARENTS MAY EXPERIENCE AN OCCASIONAL HEADACHE: THE CURE

The Institute for Adult Children of Jewish Parents utilizes a pragmatic two-step treatment plan to deal with ACoJPs with health-related concerns. Step one is

Whom Do You Know: Creating a Directory of Health Professionals.

Since many ACoJPs find it as troubling to *anticipate* being sick as to actually *be* sick, we strongly recommend that each ACoJP compile the following document.

Make a list of anyone in your family who is in a health-related profession. This should include physicians (including medical and premedical students), nurses, optometrists, veterinarians, dentists, medical technicians, journalists who specialize in medical subjects, medical secretaries, chiropractors, even local ambulance squad volunteers.

Next, systematically go through your Rolodex and/or address book and add to your list the names of all physicians you know socially, all close friends who are married to physicians, all more casual friends who are married to physicians, and all friends who are the sons/daughters of physicians or have brothers or sisters or brothers- or sisters-in-law who are physicians. Be sure to note the specialty of each.

Now (and, admittedly, this will be easiest if you are working on a computer), arrange your list by specialty. Next, begin keying your lists. Place an "A" next to any physician blood relative. Also place an "A" next to any physician you know socially. Next, place an "A – " next to the names of any very close friends married to physicians and a "B" next to the names of more casual friends married to physicians. Brother-in-law or sister-in-law physicians also rate "B." Next to the names of all friends who are the children of physicians or have brothers or sisters or brothers-in-law or sisters-in-law (or children yet!) who are physicians, place the rating "C." All other miscellaneous family sources rate "C," with the exception of chiropractors, whose rating is "D −."

As you have undoubtedly intuited by now, this directory can be an extremely important part of an ACoJP's health-maintenance arsenal. It is supremely useful during times of ill health: each "A" represents someone you can call on readily for care or a caring referral; each "B," a somewhat less caring referral, and so on. After all, when it comes to dealing with the medical profession, *whom you know* often determines the quality of the care you receive.

Probably even more important to most ACoJPs, the list you compile will be extremely reassuring. Why, just looking at it has been a way to ease the headaches of some. Which leads us to step two:

The Family Health Profile and Monthly Gazette

Some diseases run in families. So you might as well trade in your free-floating anxiety for some solid fact.

To begin, list all of your relatives, on both sides of your family, living and deceased. As much as is possible, next to each relative's name write down any diseases or injuries sustained by that person and at what age. If you are lacking information, take the lists to your mother for additional information; confirm her input, if possible, by also meeting with one or more of your aunts. Since this project is time-consuming, you may want to work with an interested ACoJP cousin in recovery. Also—and this is quite important—obtain the current addresses and telephone numbers of all family members still alive. This should include second cousins. You may want to ask if any cousin has already compiled a family history; often this person will have current telephone numbers, plus information about cousins you didn't even know existed.

The basic task here is to accurately report the health/sickness history of your family. Once you have even a few telephone numbers, start calling those relatives. Tell each what you are doing, and offer to send each a copy of the completed document. Get as much specific disease information as possible. Also, while you're on the phone, ask each for additional phone numbers and addresses of relatives with whom he or she may be in contact. (This is also an excellent opportunity to find out if there are any physicians within the extended family for listing in your Health Professionals Directory.)

Once you have completed your own family's health profile, you will have at-a-glance proof of how sick your family has been and is—or isn't. This will reassure you. If, on the other hand, it depresses you, you may have to come to a few extra meetings of Adult Children of Jewish Parents and share.

And now we are ready for the next step: a newsletter. The newsletter you produce needn't be too elaborate an affair. If you or a close friend own a MAC or some generic equivalent, you might as well just lay out and produce a professional-looking document. But plain typewriting will do. Informality can be part of a newsletter's charm.

The trick is that now that you have the necessary phone numbers, you have to call each family member once a month for a health update. Do not disclose information about the health of other people in the family while you are on the phone, unless, of course, there has been a death. But save even the medical details about the death for the newsletter.

If the person with whom you are communicating reports no illnesses, ask about doctors' appointments (older relatives like to schedule two to three of these a month, just in case); the fact that the urologist found Uncle Bennie in tiptop shape is indeed news. Be sure to inquire about which prescriptions were given and any adverse drug reactions. Also, find out the names of the doctors each went to, as relatives sometimes like to share a nice physician.

Pregnancy updates are news, too, as are difficulties conceiving. If your forty-eight-year-old first cousin, married to the sixty-three-year-old, has been marching around the mid-Atlantic region, going from one fertility doctor to another, this is definitely news. And let's not forget impotence: impotence is big news.

Be careful, in recording illnesses, not to forget the ones that may be taken for granted in your family, like depression, anxiety attacks, and agoraphobia.

Weight loss or weight gain is worth reporting, too, but only in increments of twenty pounds or more. A weight loss of fifty pounds or more is worth an entire issue. "Before" and "after" photographs would be an excellent addition.

Needless to say, the potential health and related self-esteem benefits for any ACoJP doing this project are potentially enormous. But there is money to be made as well, even if the annual charge per household is a mere $12 or $15 per subscription. Of course, if you wish, proceeds from the *Health Gazette Monthly* may be donated to your family's favorite charity.

5. Adult Children of Jewish Parents Enjoy Having a Few Nice Things: The Cure

In the course of doing extensive recovery work with Adult Children of Jewish Parents, it has become evident that the reason ACoJPs need to shop so much is that certain key inner toddler needs have not been met. Consequently I have developed several techniques for coming to terms with this deficit, one of the best of which is

ACoJP Inner Toddler Work: Nurturing Your Curiosity

If you wish, you can do this exercise with a friend equally dedicated to getting in touch with his or her inner toddler. But the optimal way to do this exercise is to join an existing inner toddler workshop—specifically one offered by the Institute for Adult Children of Jewish Parents.

An essential part of the exercise requires that you locate a photograph of yourself as a toddler. If you don't wish to speak to your mother at the moment, try calling a favorite aunt or uncle; he or she is sure to have one of the few flattering shots of you during this period. Be sure to place this photograph—even if it is a snapshot—in a suitable antique sterling or silver plate frame, or something more modern but equally tasteful. You deserve to see yourself in an appropriate setting.

Now, for at least seven days before joining with your workshop group, or with your inner toddler partner, devote at least ten minutes per day to looking at the photograph. Look deeply. Try to remember what it was like to be that toddler. Try visualizing your bedroom. Try, for example, to remember being tucked into your bed there one summer evening. Try to recall your mother's voice as you said in honest confusion, "But it's still light outside!" and her sweet reply, perhaps, "When I say it's night, it's night!"

Once this visualization has been done, and you feel so much closer to that inner toddler, you will be ready to do more direct curiosity work.

To formally begin this exercise, you will want to travel to a large, interesting department store. Ideally you might want to fly to Paris and do this inner toddler work at the Galeries Lafayette. Or you could fly to London and nurture your inner toddler at Harrods.* Domestically, a Bloomingdale's would be fine, as would a Lord & Taylor's store, Neiman-Marcus, Wanamaker's, or Saks. For this exercise, avoid discount department stores and discount malls.

Allot two days for this work. Please do not bring charge cards with you, as this workshop emphasizes looking and experiencing—not buying.

It would be best to arrive as the store opens. Walk slowly to the nearest counter. The small leather goods section is usually a good place to start. Now, step up to the counter and begin: systematically pick up and examine every single item displayed on the top of the counter or on the rack beside it. If there are twenty leather change purses on the counter, for

---

*The Institute for Adult Children of Jewish Parents sponsors four possibly tax-deductible inner toddler workshop trips each year to London and/or Paris. Two of these trips coincide with the fall and spring haute couture showings. For more information about healing your inner toddler in London or Paris this year, write: Institute for Adult Children of Jewish Parents, Heal Your Inner Toddler Abroad Program, 123 East 54 Street, Suite 8D, New York, New York 10022; or call: 1-800-TSOURIS.

example, pick up each one. Feel the weight of it. Feel how soft and smooth the leather is. Look at the color. Compare the colors: hold one change purse up to the next, a navy blue one, for example, next to a teal. Note how intense the colors look when they are placed next to each other, how the color seems almost to vibrate and pulse in the intense store light. If the change purse has a zipper, open and close the zipper. Repeat this process until you have picked up and examined every accessible item at the counter.

Now move on to handbags (male ACoJPs may want to skip handbags and move on to briefcases). With proper attention, you'll find handbags fascinating. Lift and examine each one. Feel the smoothness of the leather. Open it, and examine how the clasp works. What is the lining like? Is a tiny mirror included with the purse? How many compartments are there? Open and close any zippers there may be inside. Then look at yourself in the mirror carrying this purse. Repeat this exercise with every purse within reach.

Then move on to the next counter—briefcases, perhaps, or scarves, or fine or costume jewelry. Slowly, lingeringly, repeat this same process. Pick up and examine each and every item. Savor each to the hilt. Continue until 12:30 P.M., at which time you may break for lunch. Be sure that this lunch is in a decent restaurant. Do not order wine with lunch; nothing should interfere with your Inner Toddler Curiosity Workshop. At 1:30 return to the department store you've chosen.

Continue where you left off. By this time, perhaps, you will be in designer sportswear. Again, systematically examine every item. How are the appliqués on that Escada jacket done? Examine the attractive buttons and the way the sleeves are set in. Try on the jacket. Is it fabulous? Is the color absolutely stunning on you? Imagine yourself wearing it to work. How would wearing this jacket make you feel? How would your wearing this jacket make your co-workers feel? Then put it back; this is not a shopping trip. This is a recovery trip.

And then to the Gianni Versace boutique. Repeat the procedure. And then at 3:30 P.M., it is time to rest. The remainder of your day is free, but not to be spent inside any department stores.

On day two, the procedure is repeated. Except that today

you may examine children's clothing, housewares, furniture, and designer dresses. You may want to avoid the gourmet shop, as that could introduce other, possibly unresolved issues.

At 5:00 P.M. on day two, participants gather to discuss how the experience was for them. Almost without exception, ACoJPs report that their fervor to shop is gone. They still remain curious, observant human beings—but in recovery in that particular area of their life. In fact, when told that they may return to the department store the following morning to purchase any items they feel they can't live without, virtually no one returns. The fervor, the appetite, has been sated.

Naturally, because recovery is a *process,* participants may need to repeat the workshop periodically, some as often as once every four or five weeks.

6. ADULT CHILDREN OF JEWISH PARENTS PHONE HOME ON OCCASION: THE CURE

So many Adult Children of Jewish Parents spend a substantial portion of their energy and cash trying to reconcile their relationships with their parents, we were forced to conclude that the only really sensible therapeutic approach to this problem is

The ACoJP Ultimate Reparenting Project: Parent Swapping

Our thinking is simply this: If your parents got it wrong the first time, what makes you think it's going to be any different now? In other words, your being in recovery counts for zip if your parents are not themselves in recovery. The obvious solution, therefore, is that you may need new parents.

Here's how we've been doing it at the Institute for Adult Children of Jewish Parents: For a nominal fee, interested ACoJPs are given a series of revealing psychological questionnaires to fill out. These questionnaires reflect both temperament and intelligence. These tests are then followed by a series of revealing personal interviews, where participating ACoJPs are evaluated as to

- appearance
- presence or absence of regional accent or moles
- marital status
- career achievement and/or satisfaction
- sense of humor
- annoying habits or peculiarities
- taste in clothing and accessories
- fluency in Yiddish or other second language
- hobbies and interests

A full financial evaluation is done as well.

These results are then entered into our advanced computer system, along with the results of a "Wish List" also completed by the participant. This checklist can specify certain preferences in one's new parents, such as

- wealth
- sensitivity
- a belief in endowing their children with generous trust funds
- a quiet, refined manner
- a belief that a career in the arts is to be encouraged

Regional preferences are also taken into consideration. Because of habit, some ACoJPs may continue to prefer having parents on another coast (the "three-thousand-mile solution"). Some, on the other hand, might prefer parents closer to home. And there are always those who will prefer parents with a vacation home in Antibes. . . .

Usually the computer will offer at least two sets of potential new parents, each of whom is a certified Adult Jewish Parent in recovery. ACoJPs may then interview the new parents and make their parental adoption decision at that point.*

For a complete rate schedule, simply dial the institute's parent-swapping project at 1-800-TSOURIS.

---

*If for some reason the computer fixes up an ACoJP with an inappropriate, Jewish Jukes family, all monies will be refunded. Besides, if you don't like your new parents, you can always go back to the ones you left.

Note: Beginning in June 1994, all branches of the Institute for Adult Children of Jewish Parents will offer monthly parent-swapping parties, which you may attend (with your parents) for a nominal fee.

7. ADULT CHILDREN OF JEWISH PARENTS BELIEVE THEY NEED A LITTLE IMPROVEMENT: THE CURE

Feeling better about ourselves—especially how we look—is a key part of recovery. Which is why we highly recommend

Inner Princess Di Work

For this self-image work, you will require as much real jewelry as possible. Real diamonds are particularly important. If you have diamonds of your own, go to the safe-deposit box and get everything out. (If you're nervous about carrying them through the street, or to your car, ask a friend to go to the bank with you.) If don't have diamonds, or need to supplement what you have—as you probably will—tell your mother that you've been invited to a very important UJA benefit, you're going to wear a ball gown, and can you *please* borrow her diamond brooch, her diamond cluster earrings and (if you're lucky and she has one) the sapphire-and-diamond Deco bracelet.

Call on your friends as well. If they're good friends, tell them about ACoJP inner Princess Di work; if not, tell them you have a date with John Kennedy, Jr., and ask if they'll loan you a few pieces for the occasion. You might also speak with your cousin who inherited the best jewelry. If you need to, buy a copy of *Adult Children of Jewish Parents* for her—and give it to her with these pages marked. Chances are she has the same family dynamic as you and needs inner Princess Di work, too.

Once you've gathered together as much real jewelry as you can muster, try on everything at one time. This is a preliminary trial, so lighting and and background music do not matter very much at the moment. Assess how bedecked you are. Do you have more than one diamond brooch? Are the diamonds big enough? How are you doing on bracelets? What about neck-laces? Do you have a tiara?

Chances are you may find yourself a little short in the precious gemstone department. Analyze which items you need more of: bracelets, rings, even gem-set lipstick cases and powder compacts. This is where a little ACoJP ingenuity can be quite useful.

Proceed to your nearest well-stocked newsstand. Purchase *Town & Country,* as well as British and French or Italian *Vogue.* Now, flip through the pages of each magazine, picking out the jewels that would best complement your wardrobe: yellow diamond Cartier earclips here; a nice 31.26-carat cushion-shaped "D" color VS2 Golconda diamond ring there. You get the idea. . . . Select what suits you best.

As an alternative, you might buy or borrow a copy of *The Jewels of the Duchess of Windsor* by John Calme and Nicholas Raynor, as it contains just about any jewel a girl could ever hope for.

Next, take the book or magazines, with the appropriate pages marked, to your local photocopy shop—one that makes color copies. Ask them to photocopy the items you need, reduced or enlarged to the appropriate size for you. Then cut out the jeweled copies and, if you wish, mount them to a flexible backing: construction paper usually works extremely well.

You will need, in addition, a CD or cassette by either Neil Diamond or Barry Manilow, two of the princess's personal favorites. You will also need candles, cologne or perfume in an atomizer bottle, and a large mirror.

Set aside a quiet evening either during the week or on a weekend. Unplug your phone.

Now, take a long, relaxing bubble bath. Do your hair. Put on your makeup—and get dressed. Wear something slimming and dressy.

A little champagne would be quite pleasant now. But please do not skimp on the champagne: if you can afford it, Cristal™ would be perfect.

Scent your room with some of the cologne. Put the cats in the bathroom. Now light your candles; there should be as many candles as you can manage. In the candlelight (turn off all but the most flattering lamp), with Neil or Barry singing soothingly in the background, put on your jewels. Put on every ring. Every brooch. Every necklace.

Look at yourself in the mirror. Isn't it wonderful how you sparkle? Continue. Slowly put on all the jewelry you've prepared, including the photocopied "extras."

Turn before the mirror, so you can see yourself from all angles. Have a few sips of champagne. Wiggle your arms so you can see the bracelets glint and sparkle. And now say

- Who's the little vixen who landed the prince (even if he is a dork)?
- Who's gonna get the best jewels in Europe?
- Who looks *fabulous* in just about anything she wears?
- Who is it whom the people *really* love?
- Who's gonna get the *biggest*, fattest settlement *ever?*

Then answer

- I am!

If you wish, you may now barf.

8. Adult Children of Jewish Parents Are Quite Supportive of One Another: The Cure

One of the defining characteristics of Adult Children of Jewish Parents is their *penchant* for the sarcastic comment. Usually this comment is at someone else's expense, such as "Right, she's such a beauty, I'm sure every producer in Hollywood is waiting for her. . . ."

These sarcastic comments can be divided into two distinct types: the *external monologue*—comments said out loud, which other people can hear; and the *internal monologue*. As an example of the latter, imagine that a friend has just bought an antique *tsatske*. "It's Meissen," she says proudly. You pick it up, look at it, and a voice inside quips unexpectedly: "It *lay* next to Meissen. . . ."

For the sake of clarity, we will refer to the source of these ongoing monologues as

The Stand-Up Comic Within

There are some who claim that this little quipster within is the voice of Mother. But at the Institute for Adult Children of Jewish Parents, we believe that Mother couldn't possibly be so mean.

Naturally, few of us would want to tamper with our ability to make others laugh. But the incessant chatter of the stand-up comic within can get hard to take, especially when the quipster begins a routine during a sedate business meeting or while you're having sex—and you begin to laugh.

Therefore, as an Adult Child of Jewish Parents, you may want to do some

Inner Stand-Up Comic Work

At the core of the "stand-up comic within" dynamic, as implied above, is a certain lack of charity about the figure faults, character defects, marriages, culinary and/or erotic skills, and lapses of taste of others. The real problem is that these comments have become automatic responses over which you have no control—all too often slipping right off your tongue before you have time to either censor or control them.

That's why during the early days of your recovery—and again, periodically, every few months—it is an excellent idea to keep a running diary of both your uncharitable thoughts and your uncharitable comments.

Begin by carrying your diary with you at all times. Be sure that every time one of those fast sarcastic comments slips out, you make a note of it. Say you're at work, in a meeting with your boss and an account executive you regard (on the basis of plentiful evidence) as stupid. If, before you can help it, "Talking to her is like talking to a block of wood," slips out—well, write it down. Even if your mother calls to tell you that your sister's husband, Ed, the computer genius, got a promotion, and you think something rather benign, like Smelly Ed, right, such a bargain—write that down. Be quite thorough and complete.

Be sure that you maintain your list during business meetings, while sitting at your desk, and during and after dinner with colleagues or friends. An especially fecund opportunity for inner stand-up comic record keeping would be during family get-togethers. Just don't be abashed about your note taking.

At the end of each day, go over your list of snide comments. Ask yourself: Was this remark "Self-Serving"? Or was I simply making an "Objective Observation"? Create a chart. On the left-hand side, the heading will be "Self-Serving." The right-hand column will be headed "Objective Observation." If you wish, computerize these lists.

As you will notice, some few of your comments will, upon analysis, seem a bit self-serving. Most, however, will be objective observations.

Was it, after all, self-serving to note that chubby Cousin Rachel's wedding dress made her look as if she were wearing a lamp shade? Of course not; that was an objective observation. Was it self-serving to notice that Cousin Diane's recent foray into plastic surgery made her look as if she'd had her nose cut off? No, not at all; that too would have been objective observation. On the other hand, your rather mean-spirited quip that Cousin Ellen's new beau "couldn't be any shorter if he were a pancake" may conceivably be self-serving; after all, shortness is nothing to criticize—and besides, everyone knew that *your* escort was your gay friend Bill.

But be that as it may. If you wish, you can continue these lists indefinitely; they have been known to make amusing reading. Or, as part of your recovery, why not try to go for one waking hour each day without an uncharitable quip? Admittedly this can be a difficult task. Then, if you feel up to it during week two, try to go for two hours each day. Just don't overdo your efforts; biting humor is undoubtedly part of your charm.

Besides, given that acerbic remarks are the everyday currency of ACoJP speech, you may want to keep some in reserve for the invocation of

Curses and Invocations of the Evil Eye Workshop

ACoJPs generally believe that anyone who does them wrong will, during the offender's lifetime, suffer some serious comeuppance. For example: A woman—an employer, say—who was mean to an ACoJP and whose worst fear is that she will lose her husband to another woman, will, sooner or later, lose her husband to another woman. This is not an exaggeration; it is a statement of fact. Or another fellow, who is inordinately fond of and misuses his power in a way that does damage to an ACoJP, will quite precipitously lose his job—and his power. Another given.

It's not so much that ACoJPs *wish* others harm; it's just that that's the way things happen. Let's look at the case of Miriam S., for example, Miriam S. is a widely published author as well as an ACoJP in recovery:

About fifteen years ago, a friend of mine published her first story in The New Yorker. *I was writing short stories at the time, too, so with my friend's consent, I retyped a couple of them and excitedly sent them off to my friend's editor. Within a few weeks I received a handwritten note from my friend's editor, saying she had read the stories—and not only were they bad, I really should give up writing. Naturally I was upset. I was so upset that I never said a word to my friend about it. But then, just a short time later, I heard that the editor, a relatively young woman, died suddenly of a massive cerebral hemorrhage. . . . Let me ask you: Do you honestly think this was just a coincidence?*

Perhaps Miriam is mistaken in her reasoning—or perhaps not. These things do seem to happen. Therefore you may want to create your very own

ACoJP Hit List

Write down up to ten names of people who have done you wrong and to whom you might wish some harm. Pretend that you have access to and can afford the very best and most discreet hit man or hit woman in the world. Then try to think of creative ways to do in one or more of the people on your list.

For a person whose weakness is potato chips, for example, you might consider a gift delivery from the bar at the Carlyle Hotel of potato chips laced with undetectable poison. For someone with serious asthma, consider a decorative pillow stuffed with dog and cat hair. You get the idea. Let your imagination be your guide.

Once you have made your list and are suitably impressed by your own gift for malice, tear up the list and throw it away. This will purge many of your most uncharitable thoughts. And, should they remain . . . write it up as a murder mystery novel.

9. ADULT CHILDREN OF JEWISH PARENTS HAVE HIGHLY DEVELOPED COMMUNICATION SKILLS: THE CURE

Because Adult Children of Jewish Parents feel things so deeply, they rarely forget—or forgive—(what they see as) a slight, a criticism, a rebuff, or a betrayal. It's the kind of thing they like to reminisce about late at night, when they're having a little trouble sleeping.

Even friendships of many years may be affected. That's because Adult Children of Jewish Parents like to save things up. A bit of competitive behavior around a ski instructor during a vacation in Steamboat Springs five years ago may suddenly, during that late-night cogitation, connect with a bit of behavior in the Hamptons even longer ago than that. Add a perceived slight of the past day, or week, or month, and the result: that special ACoJP anger.

The problem, of course, is that Adult Children of Jewish Parents tend to believe that

Anger Is Forever

Given that ACoJPs have grown up in a social/family system that accepts as normal the tradition of sitting *shiva* for a relative who, say, marries out of the religion or otherwise displeases his or her parents, it's no wonder they act the way they do. They simply stop speaking to the other person involved. Some ACoJPs feel compelled to precede this act with a few snide or blunt comments, or with a note that arrives quite unexpectedly in the mail. But, on the whole, for Adult Children of Jewish Parents, the modus operandi is simply to stop speaking to or having anything to do with the offending person. For ten or twenty years at a time.

That's why, at the Institute for Adult Children of Jewish Parents, we place particular emphasis on learning to vent our anger in a more constructive way—and on trying to mend all those emotional fences.

Petaka* Practice

Make a list of five of the people with whom you've stopped speaking during, say, the past eight years. If you are participating in an institute workshop, give that list to your facilitator (along with your check). If you prefer to do your petaka work at home in an unsupervised setting, try to find a time when no one else will be at home. If you have one or more cats, put them in another room, with the door closed. If you have a dog, you might want to ask a friend to watch him or her for the afternoon or evening; otherwise, be sure that your dog is in another room, with the door securely closed. Do not do this exercise—no matter how much you may need it—with small children in the house.

On a couch or bed, place five pillows, each labeled with the name of a person with whom you no longer speak. If you have not purchased a petaka from your local Institute for Adult Children of Jewish Parents, or from your local recovery movement supply shop, roll an old towel around the thick part of a baseball bat (a child's plastic bat would be just right), and tie it securely to the bat with a stout cord. Get all breakables out of the way. Take the phone off the hook so that you won't be interrupted (call your mother first so that she won't phone the police when she can't reach you).

Before you begin, concentrate on the one person with whom you are currently angriest. Think of everything he or she did during all those years to upset you. Recall the time at a party when she told a man who was about to take your number,

*Petaka—A padded bat used during some recovery workshops for venting frustration and anger.

"Yeah, she's a stockbroker. But she just lost $120,000 in a bad deal!" Think about the time she greeted some good news of yours with, "Wow, now if you could just knock off that extra twenty pounds . . ." That's it. Think of every annoying thing she ever did. Nothing is too petty. Nothing is too small. Think about the time she marched into your apartment with white-blond hair and said with absolute seriousness, "The sun did it." Or the time she showed up to go antiquing dressed like Astor's pet horse, when she knew you were going to wear sweatpants and no makeup. Are you getting angry yet? That's it.

Go with your anger. Get into it. Now, pick up your petaka and hit the pillow marked with your friend's name. Don't be frightened or intimidated. It won't hit you back. Hit the pillow again. And again. Isn't that wonderful? Doesn't it feel good? This time, hit it again and say, "You liar! Your hair looks like straw! That color makes you look hard, and cheap!" Say it: "You look old! You have ripples in your thighs!" Say whatever comes into your mind. No insult is too horrible. Yell it. Yell it all. Yell everything you bit your tongue not to say when you were friends. Now say what you really think about your friend's boyfriend. That's it! Hit that pillow! Let it all out!

And then take a break for some ice cream. Rum raisin is quite good at a time like this. Rest a while. Perhaps you could use the pillow with your friend's name on it to prop your head. Then begin again, with a different person. Your cousin Sharon, for example, or your brother Steve.

Continue this exercise, being sure to stop for ice cream after each petaka session.

Don't you feel better?

ACoJP Family and Peer Group Reconciliation

Intrafamilial feuds, although of no particular inconvenience most of the year, can be extremely hard on the hostess planning a wedding, Bar or Bat Mitzvah, or even a seder. Therefore, as a matter of common courtesy, it behooves Adult Children of Jewish Parents to at least *try* to patch things up before an important family event.

Make a list of relatives with whom you are currently feuding.

This list should include both types of family feuds: *the declared feud,* in which you, the party involved, and everyone else know there's bad blood; and *the undeclared feud,* wherein some time ago you decided to have as little as possible to do with a certain cousin, say, because he or she tended to make you angry, upset, or still wore fur coats.

Now, make a separate list for each feudee of what exactly you have against that person. Allot at least one hour the first day to work on this assessment and between one-half and three-quarters of an hour the second day. Be specific: perhaps that person didn't approve of your first husband, so she always addressed cards to you using your maiden name; or the barbed comments another cousin made were exactly like her mother's—and you always hated her mother. Or perhaps you have a much longer grudge list: you might feel that everyone has paid attention to the grandchildren and treated you, their mother, like the maid; or everyone in your husband's family gives you, as you see it, crummy gifts; or even though your brother-in-law owns a chain of children's toy stores, when you ordered the Jungle Gym for your son, his nephew, he charged you full retail price.

Once you've completed all your lists, put them away in a safe place. Once you have defined what you are angry about, it is time to forgive.

Begin by writing a brief, nice note to each relative with whom you are feuding. Say that you're looking forward to Cousin Franklin's wedding, and wouldn't it be nice if that happy event could take place amid family harmony. Say that you'd like to patch up, as much as possible, the misunderstandings between you, and that you'll be calling in a few days' time.

Then call when you said you would. If that relative hangs up, just understand that he or she is an Adult Child of Jewish Parents—and not in recovery. Send that relative a copy of this book; he/she needs it.

Providing the relative stays on the phone—even if he or she is cold as ice, which is predictable ACoJP behavior—be nice and be succinct. Say that you want to let bygones be bygones and restore some peace to the family. Say you know you may never be as close as you once were, but you are still, after all, relatives—and blood is thicker than water. Plus, you'd like to know that if, God forbid, anything happened, you could count on that person. That's the part that will get him or her: ACoJPs feel quite flattered, self-important, and satisfied when called upon to help cope with the details of an emergency, particularly emergencies relating to health—especially the "making the phone calls to notify everyone" part.

Now you will be able to go to the wedding or Bar Mitzvah and sit anywhere, not at a special table on the other side of the room, as far away as possible from your father's sister, Aunt Carol. Your hostess will be very grateful. You can have a good time (or at least as good a time as one can have in a room full of your father's relatives). And you may actually have made peace in the family.

If, after the important event, you decide that Aunt Carol is such a sick, destructive woman that if you never see her again you'll feel nothing but relief, simply take out the note detailing all her faults, all the reasons you were angry at her in the first place, and mail it to her.

10. ADULT CHILDREN OF JEWISH PARENTS HAVE A DEEP SENSE OF COMMUNITY AND CIVIL AWARENESS: THE CURE

Sammy Davis, Jr., was not the first Jewish person in show business to marry out of his or her religion. But it is the proliferation of this practice into the lives of everyday citizens that is such a cause for concern.

In order to raise your consciousness on this issue—and aid your ACoJP recovery—please set aside a half hour to an hour of uninterrupted time. You will need a pen or pencil, writing paper, and a few refreshments.

At the top of the page, write your name. Under it write

My Personal Hybridization Profile

Now think back. . . . At what age did you begin dating? Please write that down; also indicate what year that was.

Divide the paper into three columns, as illustrated below:

129

My Personal Hybridization Profile

Began dating: *Age* _____
            Year _____

A. *Dated*	**B.** *Had Sex With*	**C.** *Married*

In column A write down the name of every person you've ever dated. It helps if you try to remember in chronological order. If you can't recall a particular name, write something you do remember, like "Laugh like a horse whinnying."

In column B write down the name of every person with whom you've ever slept. If you can't remember a particular name, write down some detail you do remember, like "Tennessee; long-distance trucker."

In column C write down the name of each person you've married.

Once you feel that you have, as nearly as possible, completed your lists, write a "J" next to each Jewish person in each list. Count the total number of Js in each list.

Good. Now call your CPA, or a mathematics teacher of your acquaintance, and ask him or her to work out the percentages for you. For example, if you've dated thirty people, and fifteen were Jewish, that would mean that 50 percent of the people you've dated were Jewish, 50 percent were "Others." If you've slept with, say, four people—given that your mother may read this book, we are deliberately conservative in this estimate— and three were "Others," that would mean that 75 percent of the people with whom you've slept have been "Others." If both people you've married have no Js next to their names, that means that 100 percent of the people you've married have been "Others."

Naturally, your own calculations may not be as straightforward as these—hence our recommendation that you seek professional assistance.

How to Assess What Your Percentages Mean

Columns A and B—Any score more than 20 percent "Others" indicates a problem. If you are currently single, you need to join a synogogue with a singles program.
Column C—Listen to your mother: you'll marry a Jewish person, you'll get a good gift. . . .

11. ADULT CHILDREN OF JEWISH PARENTS ARE RELAXED AND CASUAL IN THEIR RELATIONSHIPS WITH OTHERS: THE CURE

In order to deal with your parents' ongoing struggle for control over your life—and the lives of others—it is important that you accurately understand their special language.

WHAT THEY SAY IS NOT WHAT THEY MEAN
Jewish Parents—A Translation Guide

What They Say	What They're Really Saying
I wouldn't want to interfere.	A good daughter/son would do what I tell her/him.
My son married a controlling woman.	The shiksa. But I bite my tongue, so that I can keep seeing my grandchildren.
Who am I to say?	I am the Power.
What's to do?	Through a concentrated barrage of guilt-invoking phone calls and, if they'll let me, personal visits, I will, from this moment on, wear down their resolve until they do what I want.
No, my younger son never married.	He lives with that *feygele*, Alonso. At least they're rich, not like your son and his fat slob wife, Harriet.
We stopped for coffee.	And eggs, home fries, bagels, toast, butter, jam.

I asked her not to bring me any home fries.

I hear she gained a little weight.

So, I hear her husband left her. . . .

Your father's always been a good boy. He never gambled, he never drank, he never ran around with women.

You'll go, you'll sit, you'll talk, you'll have a little something.

They came, I ate.

Finally. I've been waiting for this.

Oy, I hope she doesn't get a better settlement than my Sheila. . . .

He did what I told him to do. You should be so lucky.

You'll go, you'll sit, you'll talk about people in a critical way, you'll have a little something.

12. Adult Children of Jewish Parents Believe That Guilt Has Taken Quite a Bad Rap. The Cure.

Recent therapeutic thinking emphasizes the importance of shame—as opposed to guilt. Which is why you may want to know

Is It Guilt—Or Is It Shame?

Scenario 1—You sit down to a typical dinner with your family. The main course is a nice, greasy brisket, accompanied by Del Monte canned creamed corn and overcooked broccoli. Just as you're about to dig in you realize that your dad has gone to the refrigerator and gotten out the leftover spaghetti from two days ago—which he then proceeds to eat, cold, as *his* main dish. He's an economical person, so you've seen him do this kind of thing before. Nevertheless, that twinge you feel, is it guilt? Is it shame? Or is it something else?

How to Tell the Difference

1. Ask yourself: Did I feel that I was being selfish to enjoy a hot, nutritious meal—while my dad, to save a few cents, has decided (again) to eat cold leftovers?

If the answer is "yes"—you were feeling guilt.

2. Or ask yourself: Did I enjoy my meal enough to reach for heaping seconds—only to meet my father's eyes . . . and suddenly feel like a worm?

If the answer is "yes"—you were feeling shame.

3. Or did you simply feel that your father was off the beam for eating the leftovers for dinner instead of lunch—and for not at least sticking them in the microwave?

If you answered "yes"—you already know the answer: You are an unfeeling, ungrateful daughter or son.

Scenario 2—You happen to stop by Bergdorf's just as they are having a cashmere sweater sale. You really need a new black turtleneck—so you charge one to your parents' account. Later, when you get it home and happily take it out of the tissue paper to show your mom, she gives you a pained look. That twinge you feel, is it guilt? Or is it shame?

How to Tell the Difference

1. Ask yourself: Did my mom suddenly make me feel that I was selfish to buy a cashmere sweater in Bergdorf's when there are so many people in the world who can't even afford Orlon?

If the answer is "yes"—you were feeling guilt.

2. Or ask yourself: Did I suddenly feel like a worm, to be spending my parents' money on a cashmere sweater when they're already pinching pennies to pay for my brother's medical school?

If the answer is "yes"—you were feeling shame.

As you will note, the operative sensation that differentiates guilt from shame is that *you feel like a worm.*

Now think back. . . . Has it been guilt you've been experiencing all these years? Of course not. You've just felt like a worm. . . .

IX

The 12 Steps for Adult Children of Jewish Parents

1. Call your mother.

2. Admit that you are powerless over your neurosis and anxiety—and that your life has become unmanageable.

3. Believe that a Power greater than your own can restore you to sanity.

4. Make a decision to turn your will and your life over to the care of that Higher Power: your mother.

5. Make a merciless inventory of the physical, intellectual, and personality flaws of yourself, everyone you've ever met, and the people on TV.

6. Humbly ask Mother to tell you exactly how and where you've gone wrong.

7. Make a list of all relatives and friends with whom you're currently not speaking, and be willing to make amends by restoring limited contact with them.

8. Buy and send a nice gift to all the people with whom you haven't been speaking. Also send a gift to the author of this book.

9. Continue your merciless inventory of your own physical, intellectual, and personality failings. Be sure to analyze where your career and marriage(s) have gone wrong.

10. Make an appointment to see a psychotherapist.

11. Seek through meditation, cooking, and cleaning the home to improve your conscious contact with Mother—seeking only for knowledge of Her will for you and the power to carry that out.

12. Visit your mother.

X

In Summation

- You are entitled.

- If it's not worth having in multiples, it's not worth having.

- You can't be too rich.

- More is, has always been, and will always be, more.

- Psychotherapy costs.

- Never stand when you can sit.

- Control can be fun.

- Anger is forever.

- If God had wanted us to diet, She/He wouldn't have invented liposuction.

- Have a nice snack.

- Diamonds are important.

- Let go and let Mother.

APPENDIX

You're Entitled!
The Adult Child of Jewish Parents Lexicon

arushi A key concept: that which you will inherit.

baleboosteh The kind of woman who cleans the bathroom and kitchen floors on her hands and knees. Joan Crawford, for example, was a *baleboosteh*.

bris Circumcision; your first family party.

bubkes What you've inherited when your brother's kids get an annuity and you get the cat.

catch (noun) A fiancé who is an M.D. or L.D.

chazzer A pig; someone who eats all the Häagen-Dazs before you get home.

chutzpah What Alan Dershowitz has, to have tried to get Imelda Marcos off. What Imelda Marcos has, to have said, "I was shopping for my country."

dreck McDonald's™; Jack in the Box™; frozen matzoh balls; Home Shopping Club; cubic zirconia.

entitled That which you deserve (only the best). Thus: I am, therefore I am entitled.

fancy (fancy schmancy) Cousin Judith, who married the transplant surgeon; Princess Michael of Kent.

feygele A male homosexual person; your husband or son. Formerly pejorative.

gonif An individual who, through subterfuge or with a gun, steals your money; an arbitrageur.

goy Any person who is not an Adult Child of Jewish Parents.

J.A.P. Someone who believes he/she is entitled. And often is.

kishke A magnificent delicacy, incorrectly known as stuffed derma; the area that hurts when you have *real* aggravation.

kishke grinder A *very* bad day at the office.

klutz A person who is a little lacking in the grace department.

kvell That which your mother will do if you marry or become a doctor.

maven An acknowledged expert. Your aunt Estelle, for example, who can tell a good diamond when she sees it, even without a loupe.

mazel Good luck; your reward for having bought this book.

mensh A person who calls his or her mother every day.

meshuggener A person who does not call his or her parents for weeks at a time.

mitzvah A wagon, sponsored by the Lubavitchers, that travels around Manhattan urging female Jews to light candles on the Sabbath eve.

M.O.T. Who wants to know?

naches What you will get more of for having bought this book.

orthopedic oxfords Practical yet unattractive footwear to enhance one's fourth-grade social standing; Jewish "Mary Janes."

oy An excellent way of expressing concern.

payess Extremely long sideburn locks, wound into Shirley Temple curls. Favored by Hasidim.

putz Mario Cuomo, for not having accepted nomination to the U.S. Supreme Court; Clarence Thomas, for having done so.

schlock What's left at Loehmann's when you've completed your shopping; Sears; Wal-Mart.

shikker Someone who has just started to read the wrong 12 Step Program.

shiksa Your sister-in-law.

shlep What you do when you can't wait for the store to deliver.

shlump A person who appears in public looking less than his or her best.

shmatte What you've been wearing in the house lately.

shpilkes Ants in your pants.

tsatske Objet d'art

tsouris Serious aggravation.

whiplash The down payment on a condo.

yentas The women with whom your mother plays or played mah-jongg. Cindy Adams; Erica Jong.

zaftig Extremely well fed.

ABOUT THE AUTHOR

Anna Sequoia, an Adult Child of Jewish Parents if ever there was one, is the author of *The Official J.A.P. Handbook, 67 Ways to Save the Animals,* and six other books. She divides her time between Greenwich Village, where's she's lived off and on for twenty years; the Bronx, where she goes for a good meal; and Taos, New Mexico, where she never stands when she can sit.